hide
this
italian
phrase
book

APA Publications GmbH & Co. Verlag KG
New York   London   Singapore

Hide This Italian Phrase Book

Contacting the Editors
Every effort has been made to provide accurate information in this publication, but changes are inevitable. The publisher cannot be responsible for any resulting loss, inconvenience or injury. We would appreciate it if readers would call our attention to any errors or outdated information by contacting Berlitz Publishing by e-mail at: comments@berlitzpublishing.com

All Rights Reserved
© 2007 APA Publications (UK) Ltd.

Printed in China by CTPS, November 2011

Writer: Nadja Rizutti
Publishing Director: Mina Patria
Commissioning Editor: Kate Drynan
Editorial Assistant: Sophie Cooper
Senior Editor/Project Manager: Lorraine Sova
Editor: Emily Bernath
Cover and Interior Design: Wee Design Group, Blair Swick
Production Manager: Raj Trivedi
Illustrations: Kyle Webster, Amy Zaleski

Distribution
Worldwide
APA Publications GmbH & Co. Verlag KG (Singapore branch), 7030 Ang Mo Kio Ave 5, 08-65 Northstar @ AMK, Singapore 569880 Email: apasin@singnet.com.sg

UK and Ireland
Dorling Kindersley Ltd., (a Penguin Company) 80 Strand, London, WC2R 0RL, UK
Email: sales@uk.dk.com

US
Ingram Publisher Services, One Ingram Blvd, PO Box 3006, La Vergne, TN 37086-1986
Email: customer.service@ingrampublisher services.com

Australia
Universal Publishers, PO Box 307, St. Leonards NSW 1590
Email: sales@universalpublishers.com.au

INSIDE

INTRO

So, you're going to an Italian-speaking country, huh? Well then, you'd better learn a couple of useful phrases. By "useful" we mean the lingo you need to hook up, check in, and hang out. This un-censored phrase book's got you covered with everything you need to speak cool Italian—saying hi, getting a room, spending your bucks, finding a cheap place to eat, scoring digits…and a helluva lot more. We've even thrown in a few totally offensive, completely inappropriate, and downright nasty terms—just for fun. You'll be able to easily spot these by looking for ▯ . Wanna know the best of the worst? Look for ▮ .

We've got your back with insider tips, too. Check these out for up-to-date info that'll help you maneuver around an Italian locale…

FACT   cool facts that may seem like fiction

the scoop   tips on what's hot and what's not

yo!   info you've gotta know

Warning—this language can get you into trouble. If you wanna say it in public, that's up to you. But we're not taking the rap (like responsibility and liability) for any problems you could encounter by using the expressions in *Hide This Italian Phrase Book*. These include, but are not limited to, verbal and/or physical abuse, bar brawls, cat fights, arrest…Use caution when dealing with Italian that's hot!

SPEAK UP

We don't want you to sound like a loser when speaking Italian. So, to make it easy for you, we've provided really simple phonetics (those are the funky letters right under the Italian expressions) with every entry you could say out loud. Just read the phonetics as if they're English:

What's up?   ← *This is English, obviously.*

Che si dice?   ← *A very cool Italian expression...*

keh see <u>dee</u>-cheh   ← *Say this as if it's English. Easy, right?!*

See this underline? That means you've gotta stress this part of the word.

stress?

If you wanna read the Italian without checking out the phonetics, remember to stress the next to last syllable unless you see an accent; if that's the case, stress the accented vowel.

sex

Meaning gender... Words in Italian can be masculine or feminine. You'll see ♂ for masculine words and ♀ for the ladies.

Yeah, baby! Now you're ready for some Italian action.

hi there

Make a good impression on the locals from the get-go.

Hi!	**Ciao!** *chah-oh* *The classic.*
Good morning!	**Buongiorno!** *bwohn-johrnoh* *Start your day by greeting the locals with class.*
Good afternoon / evening.	**Buonasera.** *bwohnah-sehrah* *Use this after lunch til late at night.*
Look who's here!	**Ma guarda chi si vede!** *mah gwahrdah key see vehdeh* *Say it when you bump into someone you haven't seen in a long time.*
How're you doing?	**Come va?** *kohmeh vah* *Simple, but still very popular.*
What's going on?	**Che mi racconti?** *keh me rahk-kohntee* *Literally: What do you want tell me?*
So...? What's up?	**Allora...? Che si dice?** *ahl-lohrah... keh see dee-cheh* *Literally: What do you say?* *You'll hear "allora" a lot!*
How are you?	**Come stai?** *kohmeh stah-ee* *Be formal; say, "Come sta?"*

1

FACT

"Ciao!" is an informal, universal expression, meaning both hi and bye. Use it frequently and you'll fit in with the "italiano" crowd.

the scoop

When meeting someone for the first time, knowing the right body language is just as important as saying the right phrases. In Italy, people traditionally greet each other by shaking hands and with a kiss on each cheek. Nowadays, this is done only with relatives and the elderly. Want to be fashionable? Drop the hand-shake and just kiss on each cheek. Afraid to get too close? A hand-shake is a safe, though standard, alternative to puckering up.

what's up

Mix and match these conversation starters.

Questions. . .

Is everything fine?	**Tutto bene?** *toot-toh behneh*
Hey, how're things?	**Ehi, come butta?** *eh-ee kohmeh boot-tah*
Hey! How's life?	**Ehi! Come ti va la vita?** *eh-ee kohmeh tee vah lah veetah*

Answers. . .

Wonderful!	**Sto da favola!** stoh dah _fahvohlah_ _Literally: I'm in a fairy tale!_
I'm fine, thanks.	**Bene, grazie.** _behneh grahtzee-eh_
Everything's OK.	**Tutto a posto.** _toot_-toh ah _pohstoh_
I feel like shit.	**Sto di merda.** stoh dee _mehrdah_

hey you!

Wanna get someone's attention? Try these.

Hey beautiful!	**A bello♂! / A bella♀!** ah _behl_-loh / ah _behl_-lah _You'll hear this a lot in Rome._ _If you want to sound like a local,_ _shout it._
Hey you!	**Ehi, tu!** _eh_-ee too _A casual way to get someone_ _to notice you. If you wanna be_ _formal, say, "Ehi, Lei!"_
Excuse me?	**Scusa?** _skoozah_ _Be polite—say "Scusi?" instead._
May I (get past)?	**Permesso?** pehr_mehs_-soh _Need to get through a mob of_ _people? Use this._

sorry

Oops…need to apologize?

Sorry! **Sono spiacente!**
sohnoh spee-ah<u>cheh</u>nteh
Formal and polite.

It was an accident. **È stato un incidente.**
eh <u>stah</u>toh oon eenchee-<u>deh</u>nteh

huh?

What did he or she just say? Make sure you understood it correctly!

Could you speak **Può parlare più lentamente?**
more slowly? *poo-<u>oh</u> pahr<u>lah</u>reh pew lehntah-<u>meh</u>nteh*
*If you're with friends, use the casual
"puoi" instead of the formal "può".*

Could you repeat that? **Può ripetere?**
poo-<u>oh</u> reepeh-tehreh

Huh? **Prego?**
<u>preh</u>goh
*"Prego" has many meanings; you
can use it to say you're welcome
or please (as in, after you).*

What was that? **Cosa ha detto?**
<u>koh</u>zah ah <u>deht</u>-toh

Could you spell it? **Come si scrive?**
<u>koh</u>meh see <u>skree</u>-veh

Please write it down. **Lo scriva, per piacere.**
loh <u>skree</u>-vah pehr pee-ah<u>cheh</u>reh

4

Can you translate this for me?	**Me lo traduce?** *meh loh trahdoocheh*
What does *this / that* mean?	**Cosa significa *questo / quello*?** *kohzah seenyee-feekah kwehstoh / kwehl-loh*
Do you speak English?	**Parla inglese?** *pahrlah eenglehzeh* *In case you couldn't understand a word he or she just said, it's OK to ask if he or she speaks your language.*
Does anyone here speak English?	**C'è qualcuno qui che parla inglese?** *cheh kwahl-koonoh kwee keh pahrlah eenglehzeh* *Use this when you're really desperate to find out what's going on.*
I don't speak (much) Italian.	**Non parlo italiano (molto bene).** *nohn pahrloh eetahlee-ahnoh (mohltoh behneh)* *Come on, we know you speak a little!*
I don't understand.	**Non capisco.** *nohn kahpeeskoh*
Do you understand?	**Capisce?** *kahpeesheh*

help

Got yourself into a sticky situation?

Can you help me?	**Mi può aiutare?** *me poo-oh ahyou-tahreh*
Help!	**Aiuto!** *ahyoutoh*

5

Go away!	**Vattene!**
	vaht-tehneh
Call the police!	**Chiami la polizia!**
	key-_ah_mee lah pohleet_zee_-ah
Stop thief!	**Al ladro!**
	ahl _lah_droh
Fire!	**Al fuoco!**
	ahl foo-_oh_koh
I'm lost.	**Mi sono perso♂ / persa♀.**
	me _soh_noh _pehr_soh / _pehr_sah
I'm sick.	**Sto male.**
	stoh _mah_leh
Get a doctor!	**Chiami un dottore!**
	key-_ah_mee oon doht-_toh_reh

emergency

Just in case you get into trouble…

Where's the police station?	**Dov'è il commissariato?**
	dohv_eh_ eel kohm-mees-sahree-_ah_toh
I want to report …	**Voglio denunciare …**
	voh-lyoh dehnoon-_chah_reh
an accident.	**un incidente.**
	oon eenchee-_dehn_teh
a mugging.	**un'aggressione per rapina.**
	oonahg-grehs-see-_oh_neh pehr rah_pee_nah
a rape.	**uno stupro.**
	_oo_noh _stew_-proh
a theft.	**un furto.**
	oon _foor_toh

I need to contact the consulate.

Devo contattare il consolato.
_deh_voh kohntaht-_tah_reh eel kohnsoh-_lah_toh

bye-bye

From classic to cool, here are the best ways to say good-bye.

Good-bye.

Arrivederci.
ahr-reeveh-_dehr_chee
Always appropriate.

See you again.

Alla prossima.
ahl-lah _prohs_-seemah
A classy way to let someone know you'd like to see him or her again.

See ya later!

A dopo!
ah _dohp_oh
Very casual. Use this with your closest friends.

See you!

Ci si vede!
chee see _veh_deh
Say this when you have plans to meet up again later.

Good night.

Buonanotte.
bwohnah-_noht_-teh
Said only before going to bed. The exception: if you've been partying all night and you're saying good-bye at 3 AM.

Keep in touch!

Ci sentiamo!
chee sehntee-_ah_moh
Literally: We'll hear from each other!

2 GETTIN' AROUND

by plane

Just arrived? Going somewhere? Act like you know what you're doing.

A ticket to …	**Un biglietto per …** *oon bee-lyeht-toh pehr* *Hint: If you want classic, check out Florence, Rome, and Venice. If you want country, head for the Chianti region.*
One-way.	**Di andata.** *dee ahndahtah*
Round-trip.	**Di andata e ritorno.** *dee ahndahtah eh reetohrnoh*
How much?	**Quanto?** *kwahntoh*
Are there any discounts?	**C'è una riduzione?** *cheh oonah reedootzee-ohneh* *Doesn't hurt to ask!*
When is the … flight to …?	**Quando parte … volo per …?** *kwahndoh pahrteh … vohloh pehr*
first	**il primo** *eel preemoh*
next	**il prossimo** *eel prohs-seemoh*
last	**l'ultimo** *loolteemoh*
I'd like *a ticket / two tickets*.	**Vorrei *un biglietto / due biglietti*.** *vohr-ray oon bee-lyeht-toh / doo-eh bee-lyeht-tee* *Traveling alone or with a "friend"?*

Is flight … delayed?	**C'è un ritardo sul volo …?**
	cheh oon ree<u>tahr</u>doh sool <u>voh</u>loh
	Keep your fingers crossed that it's not!

| How late will it be? | **Di quanto ritarderà?** |
| | *dee <u>kwahn</u>toh reetahr-deh<u>rah</u>* |

| Which gate does flight … leave from? | **Da quale uscita parte il volo …?** |
| | *dah <u>kwahl</u>eh oo<u>shee</u>-tah <u>pahr</u>teh eel <u>voh</u>loh* |

| Where is / Where are …? | **Dov'è / Dove sono …?** |
| | *doh<u>veh</u> / <u>doh</u>veh <u>soh</u>noh* |

| the baggage check | **il deposito bagagli** |
| | *eel deh<u>poh</u>-zeetoh bah<u>gah</u>-lyee* |

| the luggage carts | **i carrelli** |
| | *ee kahr-<u>rehl</u>-lee* |

| the lockers | **il deposito bagagli automatico** |
| | *eel deh<u>poh</u>-zeetoh bah<u>gah</u>-lyee ah-ootoh<u>mah</u>-teekoh* |

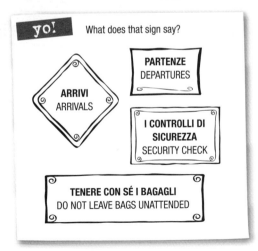

yo! What does that sign say?

PARTENZE
DEPARTURES

ARRIVI
ARRIVALS

I CONTROLLI DI SICUREZZA
SECURITY CHECK

TENERE CON SÉ I BAGAGLI
DO NOT LEAVE BAGS UNATTENDED

the Scoop

Need cheap airline tickets? Do your research online. It's not only sites like cheaptickets.com, expedia.com, and orbitz.com that offer great fares; you should also check out airline sites for special promotions. If that seems like too much work, have someone do the work for you—call a travel agent for help. A fee for research probably won't be charged.

in flight

Sit back (if possible) and enjoy.

Do you have *a blanket* / *a pillow*?	**Ha *una coperta* / *un cuscino*?** *ah oonah kohpehr-tah / oon kooshee-noh*
I ordered a … meal.	**Ho ordinato un menu …** *oh orhdee-nahtoh oon mehnoo*
diabetic	**per diabetici** *pehr dee-ahbeh-teechee*
gluten free	**senza glutine** *sehntzah glooteeneh*
kosher	**kosher** *koh-shehr*
vegan	**vegano** *vehgahnoh*
vegetarian	**vegetariano** *vehjeh-tahree-ahnoh*

I ordered a … meal.	**Ho ordinato un menu …** *oh orhdee-<u>nah</u>toh oon meh<u>noo</u>*
low-calorie	**a basso contenuto calorico.** *ah <u>bahs</u>-soh kohnteh-<u>noo</u>toh kahl<u>oh</u>-reekoh*
low-cholesterol	**a basso contenuto di colesterolo.** *ah <u>bahs</u>-soh kohnteh-<u>noo</u>toh dee kohleh-steh<u>roh</u>loh*
low-fat	**a basso contenuto di grassi.** *ah <u>bahs</u>-soh kohnteh-<u>noo</u>toh dee <u>grahs</u>-see*
low-sodium	**a basso contenuto di sodio.** *ah <u>bahs</u>-soh kohnteh-<u>noo</u>toh dee <u>sohdee-oh</u>*
I need a barf bag.	**Presto, un sacchetto di carta.** *<u>preh</u>stoh oon sahk-<u>keht</u>-toh dee <u>kahr</u>tah Gross.*

your stuff

Find it, grab it, and go!

Where is the luggage from flight …?	**Dove sono i bagagli del volo …?** *<u>doh</u>veh <u>soh</u>noh ee bah<u>gah</u>-lyee dehl <u>voh</u>loh*
My luggage has been stolen.	**Il mio bagaglio è stato rubato.** *eel <u>me</u>-oh bah<u>gah</u>-lyoh eh <u>stah</u>toh roo<u>bah</u>toh*
My suitcase was damaged.	**La mia valigia è stata danneggiata.** *lah <u>me</u>-ah vah<u>lee</u>jah eh <u>stah</u>tah dahn-neh<u>dj</u>ahtah*
My luggage hasn't arrived.	**I miei bagagli non sono arrivati.** *ee me-<u>ay</u> bah<u>gah</u>-lyee nohn <u>soh</u>noh ahr-ree<u>vah</u>tee*

by train

OK, first, you gotta get there.

How do I get to the train station?

Come si arriva alla stazione ferroviaria?
kohmeh see ahr-reevah ahl-lah stahtzee-ohneh fehr-rohvee-ahree-ah

Is it far?

È lontano?
eh lohntahnoh

waitin' for the train

Learn to negotiate your way around the station.

Where is / Where are …?

Dov'è / Dove sono …?
dohveh / dohveh sohnoh

the baggage check

il deposito bagagli
eel dehpoh-zeetoh bahgah-lyee

the bathroom

la toilette
lah twah-leht

the currency-exchange

l'ufficio cambio
loof-feechoh kahmbee-oh

the information desk

lo sportello informazioni
loh spohrtehl-loh eenfohr-mahtzee-ohnee

the lockers

il deposito bagagli automatico
eel dehpoh-zeetoh bahgah-lyee ah-ootohmah-teekoh

the lost and found

l'ufficio oggetti smarriti
loof-feechoh ohdjeht-tee zmahr-reetee

Where is / Where are …?	**Dov'è / Dove sono …?**
	dohveh / dohveh sohnoh
the pay phone	**il telefono a scheda**
	eel tehleh-fohnoh ah skehdah
the platforms	**i binari**
	ee beenahree
the snack bar	**il bar**
	eel bahr
the ticket office	**la biglietteria**
	lah bee-lyeht-tehree-ah
the waiting room	**la sala d'aspetto**
	lah sahlah dahspeht-toh
I'd like a … ticket to …	**Vorrei un biglietto … per …**
	vohr-ray oon bee-lyeht-toh … pehr
one-way	**di sola andata**
	dee sohlah ahndahtah
round-trip	**di andata e ritorno**
	dee ahndahtah eh reetohrnoh
How much is that?	**Quant'è?**
	kwahnteh
Is there a discount for students?	**C'è una riduzione per studenti?**
	cheh oonah reedootzee-ohneh pehr stew-dehntee
	You could save big bucks!
Do you offer a cheap same-day round-trip fare?	**C'è una tariffa economica per andata e ritorno in giornata?**
	cheh oonah tahreef-fah ehkoh-nohmeekah pehr ahndahtah eh reetohrnoh een johrnahtah
Could I have a schedule?	**Ha l'orario?**
	ah lohrahree-oh

When is the train to …?	**Quando parte il treno per …?**
	_kwahn_doh _pahr_teh eel _treh_noh pehr
How long is the trip?	**Quanto dura il viaggio?**
	_kwahn_toh _doo_rah eel vee-_ah_-djoh
	Prepare yourself.

train talk

Whether you're waiting for the train or looking for a seat, make casual conversation with a good-looking Italian.

Hello! Where is platform …?	**Ciao! Dov'è il binario …?**
	chah-oh doh_veh_ eel bee_nah_ree-oh
Is this the train to …?	**È questo il treno per …?**
	eh _kweh_stoh eel _treh_noh pehr
	I bet you're hoping he/she will be on your train.
Hello, hottie. Is this seat taken?	**Ciao bello♂ / bella♀. Questo posto è occupato?**
	chah-oh _behl_-lah / _behl_-loh _kweh_stoh _poh_stoh eh ohk-koo_pah_toh
	A little eye candy for the trip will make the ride seem much shorter!
Do you mind if I sit here?	**Ti dispiace se mi siedo qui?**
	tee deespee-_ah_cheh seh me see-_eh_doh kwee
	Go ahead—get closer.
Do you mind if I open the window?	**Ti dispiace se apro il finestrino?**
	tee deespee-_ah_cheh seh _ah_proh eel feeneh-_stree_noh
	Is it hot in here, or is it just you?

yo! What does that sign say?

| GABINETTI | AI BINARI |
| RESTROOMS | TO THE PLATFORMS |

| INFORMAZIONI | PRENOTAZIONI | USCITA |
| INFORMATION | RESERVATIONS | EXIT |

FACT

Italy has an extensive and pretty dependable train network. From the major rail stations you can get to just about any Italian city you want to visit. Keep in mind, though, that trains are often crowded and you may need to reserve a seat or arrive well before the scheduled departure.

by bus

It's cheap, so if you are too, this is the way to go.

Where is the bus station? | **Dov'è la stazione dei pullman?**
dohveh lah stahtzee-ohneh day pool-mahn
It's a coach or long-distance bus.
If you want a local or city bus,
it's "l'autobus".

Where can I buy tickets? | **Dove si comprano i biglietti?**
dohveh see kohmprahnoh ee bee-lyeht-tee

How much is the fare to …? | **Quant'è il biglietto per …?**
kwahnteh eel bee-lyeht-toh pehr

A … ticket to …, please.	**Un biglietto … per …, per favore.** *oon bee-lyeht-toh … pehr … pehr* *fahvohreh*
one-way	**di sola andata** *dee sohlah ahndahtah*
round-trip	**di andata e ritorno** *dee ahndahtah eh reetohrnoh*
Is this the right bus to …?	**È questo l'autobus per …?** *eh kwehstoh lah-ootohboos pehr*
Could you tell me when to get off?	**Può dirmi quando devo scendere?** *poo-oh deermee kwahndoh dehvoh* *shehndehreh* *Just in case you have no clue* *where you're headed.*
Next stop, please!	**La prossima fermata, per favore!** *lah prohs-seemah fehrmahtah pehr* *fahvohreh* *If you want the driver to stop,* *say please!*

by subway

Is goin' underground your style? Then you'll need these.

Where's the nearest subway station?	**Dov'è la fermata della metro più vicina?** *dohveh lah fehrmahtah dehl-lah mehtroh* *pew veecheenah* *Please let it be in walking distance.*
Where can I buy tickets?	**Dove si comprano i biglietti?** *dohveh see kohmprahnoh ee bee-lyeht-tee*

Could I have a subway map?	**Ha una mappa della metro?** *ah <u>oo</u>nah <u>mahp</u>-pah <u>dehl</u>-lah <u>meh</u>troh* *If you ask nicely, you may* *actually get what you want.*
Which line should I take for …?	**Che linea devo prendere per …?** *keh <u>lee</u>nehah <u>deh</u>voh <u>prehn</u>-dehreh pehr* *If the subway map is incompre-* *hensible, ask a cutie for help.*
Which stop is it for …?	**Qual è la fermata per …?** *kwah<u>leh</u> lah fehr<u>mah</u>tah pehr*
Is the next stop …?	**La prossima fermata è …?** *lah <u>prohs</u>-seemah fehr<u>mah</u>tah eh* *Wanna sound savvy despite being* *lost? Drop the word "fermata".*
Where are we?	**Dove siamo?** *<u>doh</u>veh see-<u>ah</u>moh* *Don't have a clue, huh?!*

The "metropolitana" in Rome and Milan provide large maps in every station to help you find your way around. A subway ticket has a flat fee, regardless of how far you're going. Don't forget to validate your ticket in the machines before you get on the subway. If you're caught without a validated ticket, you'll pay a hefty fine.

by taxi

Feelin' lazy? Get a cab.

Where can I get a taxi?	**Dove si trovano i tassì?** *dohveh see trohvahnoh ee tahs-see*
Please take me …	**Per favore, mi porti …** *pehr fahvohreh me pohrtee*
to a good bar.	**a un bar carino.** *ah oon bahr kahreenoh*
to a good club.	**a un bella discoteca.** *ah oonah behl-lah deeskoh-tehkah*
to a cute little bar.	**a un baretto simpatico.** *ah oon bahreht-toh seem-pahteekoh*
to the airport.	**all'aeroporto.** *ahl-lah-ehrohpohrto*
to the train station.	**alla stazione ferroviaria.** *ahl-lah stahtzee-ohneh fehr-rohvee-ahree-ah*
to this address.	**a questo indirizzo.** *ah kwehstoh eendee-reetzoh*
How much will it cost?	**Quanto costerà?** *kwahntoh kohstehrah* *Know before you go.*
How much is that?	**Quant'è?** *kwahnteh*
Keep the change.	**Il resto è per Lei.** *eel rehstoh eh pehr lay*

 **FACT** All cabs in Italy have meters, but it's still smart to ask in advance how much a long trip will cost. Expect to pay a supplement for hailing a taxi on Sundays, holidays, at night (11 p.m.–6 a.m.), and at the airport. Information about additional charges should be posted somewhere inside the taxi. If you've got any cash left over after all these fees, tip your cabbie 10–15%.

Beware of unlicensed cabs ("abusivi") at airports and train or bus stations—you'll probably be overcharged. Avoid these by catching a taxi at an official taxi stand.

by car

Can't give up the luxury of having your own car?

I'd like to rent …	**Vorrei noleggiare …** *vohr-ray nohleh-djahreh*
an automatic.	**un'auto con il cambio automatico.** *oonah-ootoh kohn eel kahmbee-oh ah-ootohmah-teekoh*
a car with air conditioning.	**un'auto con aria condizionata.** *oonah-ootoh kohn ahree-ah kohndeet-zee-ohnahtah*
How much does it cost *per day / per week*?	**Quanto costa *al giorno / alla settimana*?** *kwahntoh kohstah ahl johrnoh / ahl-lah seht-teemahnah*

Are mileage and insurance included?	**Il chilometraggio e l'assicurazione sono inclusi?**
	eel key-lohmeh-trahdjoh eh lahs-seekoorahtzee-ohneh sohnoh eenkloozee
	These can really add up.

| Where's the next gas station? | **Dov'è la prossima stazione di servizio?** |
| | *dohveh lah prohs-seemah stahtzee-ohneh dee sehrveetzee-oh* |

| Fill it up, please. | **Il pieno, per favore.** |
| | *eel pee-ehnoh pehr fahvohreh* |

car trouble

Having a breakdown?

| My car broke down. | **Ho un guasto all'automobile.** |
| | *oh oon gwahstoh ahl-lah-ootohmoh-beeleh* |

| Can you send *a mechanic / a tow truck*? | **Può mandare *un meccanico / un carro attrezzi*?** |
| | *poo-oh mahndahreh oon mehk-kah-neekoh / oon kahr-roh aht-trehtzee* |

I've run out of gas.	**Ho finito la benzina.**
	oh feeneetoh lah behndzeenah
	Duh!

| I have a flat. | **Ho forato.** |
| | *oh fohrahtoh* |

I've locked the keys in the car.	**Ho lasciato le chiavi in macchina.**
	oh lahshahtoh leh key-ahvee een mahk-keynah
	Nice one.

**FACT** Ready for a road trip? Be sure to find out before you leave if you'll need an International Driving Permit to drive in Italy. Keep an eye on speed limit signs but don't forget—that's kilometers, not miles, per hour! The last thing you need is to get pulled over by the police; in case you do, here's some useful lingo:

I had the right of way.	**Avevo la precedenza.**
	ahvehvoh lah prehcheh-dehntzah
I didn't see the sign.	**Non ho visto il segnale.**
	nohn oh veestoh eel sehnyahleh
	Excuses, excuses.
He ran into me.	**Mi ha investito lui.**
	me ah eenveh-steetoh loo-ee

by bike

Calling all bikers…

I'd like to rent …	**Vorrei noleggiare …**
	vohr-ray nohleh-djahreh
a bike.	**una bici.**
	oonah beechee
a moped.	**un motorino.**
	oon mohtoh-reenoh
a motorbike.	**una moto.**
	oonah mohtoh

How much does it cost *per day / per week*?	**Quanto costa *al giorno / alla settimana*?**
	kwahntoh kohstah ahl johrnoh / ahl-lah seht-teemahnah
	Don't get screwed; confirm the price in advance.

by thumb

Hitchhiking is NOT recommended.

Where are you heading?	**In che direzione va?**
	een keh deerehtzee-ohneh vah
Is that on the way to …?	**È sulla strada per …?**
	eh sool-lah strahdah pehr
Could you drop me off here?	**Può farmi scendere qui?**
	poo-oh fahr-mee shehndehreh kwee
Thanks for the ride.	**Grazie per il passaggio.**
	grahtzee-eh pehr eel pahs-sahdjoh
	It doesn't hurt to be nice.

 **MONEY**

get cash

Get your hands on some euros and start spending them!

Where's the nearest …?	**Dov'è … più vicino ♂ / vicina ♀?** *dohveh… pew veecheenoh / veecheenah*
ATM	**il bancomat** *eel bahn-kohmaht*
bank	**la banca** *lah bahnkah*
currency exchange office	**l'ufficio di cambio** *loof-feechoh dee kahmbee-oh*

Can I exchange foreign currency here?
Qui si può cambiare valuta straniera?
kwee see poo-oh kahmbee-ahreh vahlootah strahnee-ehrah

I'd like to change some *dollars / pounds* into euros.
Vorrei cambiare alcuni *dollari / sterline* in euro.
vohr-ray kahmbee-ahreh ahlkoonee dohl-lahree / stehr-lee-neh een eh-ooroh

I want to cash some travelers checks.
Voglio incassare dei traveler check.
voh-lyoh eenkahs-sahreh day trah-vehlehr chehk

What's the exchange rate?
Quant'è il cambio?
kwahnteh eel kahmbee-oh

If you're concerned about the changing rates, charge it—you'll get that day's rate as calculated by your credit card company.

25

How much commission do you charge?	**Quanto prendete di commissione?**
	kwahntoh prehn-dehteh dee kohm-mees-see-ohneh
	Watch out for those hidden fees.

Get the best rate for your dollars or pounds by exchanging your money at "l'ufficio di cambio", a currency exchange office. They can be found in most tourist centers and often offer better exchange rates than hotels and banks. Keep in mind that you've gotta bring your passport if you wanna change money!

ATM

Get cash fast.

Where is the ATM?	**Dove' è il bancomat?**
	dohveh eel bahn-kohmaht
Can I use my card in the ATM?	**Posso usare la mia carta al bancomat?**
	pohs-soh oozahreh lah mee-ah kahrtah al bahn-kohmaht
The ATM ate my card.	**Il bancomat si è mangiato la mia carta.**
	eel bahn-kohmaht see eh mahnjahtoh lah mee-ah kahrtah
	Good luck getting another one!

 It won't be too tough to get cash 24/7 in Italy. If you have an ATM, bank, or credit card you should be able to withdraw money from most ATMs or bank machines in cities and larger towns. If your PIN number is a word, make sure you memorize the number equivalents since many foreign ATMs don't have letters on their key pads. You'll probably get hit with some stiff fees by both your bank and the card's network (Cirrus, Explore, Interlink, Plus, Star, etc.) for accessing the International ATM System. Call your bank in advance to find out its international ATM withdrawal fees.

charge it

Can't figure out the currency exchange? Avoid the hassle and use your credit card.

Can I withdraw money on my credit card here?	**Posso fare un prelievo con la mia carta di credito?** *pohs-soh fahreh oon preh-lee-ehvoh kohn lah mee-ah kahrtah dee krehdeetoh*
Do you take credit cards?	**Accetta carte di credito?** *ah-cheht-tah kahrteh dee krehdeetoh*
I'll pay by credit card.	**Pago con carta di credito.** *pahgoh kohn kahrtah dee krehdeetoh*

 Some credit card companies charge a currency conversion fee for international purchases. Contact your bank or credit card company to find out more before you rack up any big charges.

pay up

Here's how to part with your hard-earned dough.

Where do I pay?

Dove si paga?
dohveh see pahgah

How much is that?

Quanto costa?
kwahntoh kohstah
You can also simply say "Quant'è?".

Do you have anything
on sale?

Ha delle offerte speciali?
ah dehl-leh ohf-fehrteh spehchahlee

Sorry, I don't have
enough money.

**Mi dispiace, non ho abbastanza
soldi.**
*me deespee-ahcheh nohn oh
ahb-bahstahntzah sohldee*
How embarrassing.

Could I have a receipt,
please?

Mi dà la ricevuta, per favore?
me dah lah reecheh-vootah pehr fahvohreh

VAT, value-added tax, or "IVA" in Italian, is imposed on just
about everything, so don't be shocked by the sticker price!
If you're spending a lot of money, the tax you paid can be
reclaimed when leaving Italy if you live outside the European
Union. You'll need to get the VAT refund forms directly from
participating vendors when you make your purchase. Then,
have the forms stamped by a customs official at the airport
of your departure. Happy spending!

4 HOTEL

get a room

You know you want to.

Can you recommend a hotel in …?

Può consigliarmi un albergo a …?
poo-oh kohnsee-lyahrmee oon ahlbehrgoh ah
To sound even more like a local,
say your destination in "italiano".
Florence is "Firenze"; Milan,
"Milano"; Naples, "Napoli"; Rome,
"Roma"; and Venice, "Venezia".

Is it near the center of town? **È vicino al centro?**
eh veecheenoh ahl chehntroh
You've gotta be close to where the
bars and clubs are, right?

How much is it per night? **Quanto costa a notte?**
kwahntoh kohstah ah noht-teh
Whether you're looking for something
swanky or going cheap, make sure
you know what it'll cost!

Is there anything cheaper? **C'è qualcosa di più economico?**
cheh kwahl-kohzah dee pew ehkoh-
nohmeekoh

I have a reservation.

Ho una stanza prenotata.
oh oonah stahntzah prehnoh-tahtah

My name is …

Sono …
sohnoh

I confirmed by e-mail.

Ho confermato la prenotazione
per mail.
oh kohnfehr-mahtoh lah prehnoh-tahtzee-
ohneh pehr mehl
E-mail can be translated as "mail" or
"e-mail" or even "posta elettronica".

at the hotel

Need a room for tonight? Ask the right questions.

Do you have a room?	**Avete camere libere?** *ahvehteh kahmehreh leebehreh*
I'd like a *single / double* room.	**Vorrei una camera *singola / doppia*.** *vohr-ray oonah kahmehrah seengohlah / dohp-pee-ah*
I'd like a room with a *double bed / twin beds*.	**Vorrei una camera con *letto matrimoniale / due letti*.** *vohr-ray oonah kahmehrah kohn leht-toh mahtree-mohnee-ahleh / doo-eh leht-tee* *Get a double if you want to snuggle with someone; two twin beds if you're sick and tired of the person you're traveling with.*
I'd like a room with a *bath / shower*.	**Vorrei una camera con *bagno / doccia*.** *vohr-ray oonah kahmehrah kohn bahnyoh / dohtchah*
A non-smoking room.	**Una camera per non fumatori.** *oonah kahmehrah pehr nohn foomah-tohree*
A smoking room.	**Una camera per fumatori.** *oonah kahmehrah pehr foomah-tohree*

gotta have

Things you can't do without.

Is there (a) … in the room?	**C'è … in camera?** *cheh … een kahmehrah*
air conditioning	**l'aria condizionata** *laahree-ah kohndeetzee-ohnahtah*

31

Is there (a) … in the room?	**C'è … in camera?**
	cheh … een kahmehrah
phone	**il telefono**
	eel tehleh-fohnoh
TV	**la TV**
	lah tee-voo

Does the hotel have (a) …?	**L'albergo ha …**
	lahlbehrgoh ah
Wi-Fi® area	**l'accesso wireless a Internet**
	lah-tchehs-soh waheerlehss ah eentehrneht
internet access	**l'accesso a Internet**
	lah-tchehs-soh ah eentehrneht
swimming pool	**la piscina**
	lah peeshe-nah
restaurant	**il ristorante**
	eel reestoh-rahnteh
room service	**il servizio in camera**
	eel sehrveetzee-oh een kahmehrah

price

It all comes down to one thing.

How much is it *per night* / *per week*?	**Quant'è *a notte* / *alla settimana*?**
	kwahnteh ah noht-teh / ahl-lah seht-teemahnah
Does the price include breakfast?	**Il prezzo include la colazione?**
	eel prehtzoh eenkloodeh lah kohlahtzee-ohneh
That's fine. I'll take it.	**Va bene. La prendo.**
	vah behneh lah prehndoh

problems

Tell 'em what's bothering you.

I've lost my key.
Ho perso la chiave.
oh pehrsoh lah key-ahveh

I've locked myself out of my room.
Mi sono chiuso ♂ / chiusa ♀ fuori della camera.
me sohnoh kewzoh / kewzah foo-ohree dehl-lah kahmehrah
Nice one.

The lock is broken.
La serratura è rotta.
lah sehr-rahtoorah eh roht-tah
Seems a bit dangerous...

... doesn't work.
... non funziona.
nohn foontzee-ohnah

   The air conditioning
   L'aria condizionata
   lahree-ah kohndeetzee-ohnahtah

   The fan
   Il ventilatore
   eel vehntee-lahtohreh

   The heat
   Il riscaldamento
   eel reeskahldah-mehntoh

   The light
   La luce
   lah loocheh

I can't turn the heat *on / off*.
Non posso *accendere / spegnere* il riscaldamento.
nohn pohs-soh ah-tchehn-dehreh / spehnyehreh eel reeskahldah-mehntoh

There is no *hot water / toilet paper*.
Non c'è *acqua calda / carta igienica*.
nohn cheh ahk-kwa kahldah / kahrtah eejeh-neekah

FACT

Don't get burnt out. The 220-volt, 50-cycle AC is the norm in Italy. If you bring your own electrical gizmos overseas, you'll need to buy an adapter to fit the various types of electrical sockets. You may also need to purchase a voltage converter to keep your digital camera, hairdryer, and electric shaver from getting fried.

necessities

More importantly…

Where's the bar?	**Dov'è il bar?** *dohveh eel bahr* *This may be the most important expression in the entire book.*
Where's the swimming pool?	**Dov'è la piscina?** *dohveh lah peeshe-nah*
Where are the bathrooms?	**Dov'è il bagno?** *dohveh eel bahnyoh*
What time are the doors locked?	**A che ora chiudete?** *ah keh ohrah kewdehteh* *If you're staying at a guest house, bed and breakfast, or even a hostel, you may have a curfew!*
What time is breakfast served?	**A che ora è servita la colazione?** *ah keh ohrah eh sehrveetah lah kohlahtzee-ohneh*

Could you wake me at …?	**Può svegliarmi alle …?** *poo-oh sveh-lyahrmee ahl-leh*
I'd like to leave this in the safe.	**Vorrei mettere questo in cassaforte.** *vohr-ray meht-tehreh kwehstoh een kahs-sahfohrteh*
May I have …?	**Potrei avere …?** *pohtray ahvehreh*
a towel	**un asciugamano** *oon ahshoo-gahmahnoh*
a blanket	**una coperta** *oonah kohpehr-tah*
a pillow	**un cuscino** *oon kooshee-noh*
some toilet paper	**della carta igienica** *dehl-lah kahrtah eejeh-neekah*
Are there any messages for me?	**Ci sono messaggi per me?** *chee sohnoh mehs-sahdjee pehr meh*

hostel

Looking for budget accommodations? The language you need is right here.

Do you have any places left for tonight?	**Avete posti liberi per questa notte?** *ahvehteh pohstee leebehree pehr kwehstah noht-teh*
Do you rent out bedding?	**Noleggiate la biancheria da letto?** *nohleh-djahteh lah bee-ahnkehree-ah dah leht-toh*

35

| What time are the doors locked? | **A che ora chiudete?**
ah keh <u>oh</u>rah kew<u>deh</u>te |

| I have an International Student Card. | **Ho una Carta Internazionale dello Studente.**
oh <u>oo</u>nah <u>kah</u>rtah eentehr-nahtzee-oh<u>nah</u>leh <u>dehl</u>-loh stew-<u>dehn</u>teh |

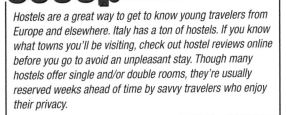

the scoop

Hostels are a great way to get to know young travelers from Europe and elsewhere. Italy has a ton of hostels. If you know what towns you'll be visiting, check out hostel reviews online before you go to avoid an unpleasant stay. Though many hostels offer single and/or double rooms, they're usually reserved weeks ahead of time by savvy travelers who enjoy their privacy.

check out

It's time to go.

| What time do we have to check out? | **A che ora dobbiamo lasciare libera la camera?**
ah keh <u>oh</u>rah dohb-bee-<u>ah</u>moh lah<u>shah</u>reh <u>lee</u>behrah lah <u>kah</u>mehrah |

| Could we leave our luggage here until …? | **Possiamo lasciare i bagagli fino alle …?**
pohs-see-<u>ah</u>moh lah<u>shah</u>reh ee bah<u>gah</u>-lyee <u>fee</u>noh <u>ahl</u>-leh
Last thing you wanna do is walk around all day with your heavy backpack! |

| The bill, please. | **Vorrei il conto, per favore.** |
| | *vohr-ray eel kohntoh pehr fahvohreh* |

| Could I have a receipt? | **Mi dà la ricevuta?** |
| | *me dah lah reecheh-vootah* |

Do you take credit cards?	**Accetta carte di credito?**
	ah-tcheht-tah kahrteh dee krehdeetoh
	Cross your fingers that they do.

I think there's a mistake.	**Penso che ci sia un errore.**
	pehnsoh keh chee see-ah oon ehr-rohreh
	Oh, really?

| I've made … telephone calls. | **Ho fatto … telefonate.** |
| | *oh faht-toh … tehleh-fohnahteh* |

I've taken … from the mini-bar.	**Ho preso … dal minibar.**
	oh prehzoh … dahl meeneebahr
	You lush.

camping

If camp is your thing, here's the info you need.

| Is there a campsite nearby? | **C'è un campeggio qui vicino?** |
| | *cheh oon kahmpehdjoh kwee veecheenoh* |

| Do you have space for a tent? | **Avete il posto per una tenda?** |
| | *ahvehteh eel pohstoh pehr oonah tehndah* |

| What is the charge *per day* / *per week*? | **Quanto costa *al giorno* / *alla settimana*?** |
| | *kwahntoh kohstah ahl johrnoh / ahl-lah seht-teemahnah* |

| Are there cooking facilities on site? | **Ci sono attrezzature per cucinare?** |
| | *chee sohnoh aht-trehtzahtooreh pehr koochee-nahreh* |

Where are the showers?	**Dove sono le docce?**
	dohveh sohnoh leh dohtcheh
	Nature sure is dirty, isn't it?!

 Think that campgrounds are for hippies only? Camping in Italy is totally common, even in urban areas like Florence, Rome, and Venice. Camp sites cost way less than hotel rooms, so sleeping in the great outdoors is a smart way to make sure that you always have money left over to party!

where to eat

What are ya in the mood for?

Let's go to …   **Andiamo a …**
                             ahndee-ahmoh ah

a restaurant.   **un ristorante.**
                             oon reestoh-rahnteh

a bar.   **un bar.**
                             oon bahr

a café.   **un caffè.**
                             oon kahf-feh

an ice-cream parlor.   **una gelateria.**
                             oonah jehlah-tehree-ah

a sandwich shop.   **una paninoteca.**
                             oonah pahnee-nohtehkah

 Italy has no lack of delicious food and you don't have to pay too much to eat like a king (or queen). Here's where to go to eat your fill without emptying your wallet.

Trattoria: This medium-priced restaurant serves meals and drinks. The food is simple, but good.

Taverna: This is a more modest type of "trattoria". Expect lower prices and not much ambiance, but the food will still be hearty and tasty.

Osteria: This inn has simple food and, more importantly, wine.

Another way to save cash is to get the "menù turistico", a fixed-price three- or four-course meal. You won't have much choice about what you eat but you'll leave with enough money to hit the clubs after dinner!

yo! Now that you know where to eat, you'd better learn *when* to eat.

la colazione
lah kohlahtzee-ohneh

Breakfast is served from 7–10 a.m. Italians usually have a cappuccino and a croissant, doughnut, or other "pezzo dolce" for breakfast.

il pranzo
eel prahndzoh

Lunch is served from 12:30–2 p.m. Be careful though— in some smaller towns, lunch is called "colazione".

la cena
lah cheh-nah

Dinner begins at 8 p.m. Get ready for a late night!

fast food

In a rush? Grab a quick bite to eat so you can keep sightseeing.

I'd like …	**Vorrei …** *vohr-ray*
a burger.	**un hamburger.** *oon ahmboorgher*
fries.	**delle patatine fritte.** *dehl-leh pahtah-teeneh freet-teh*
a sandwich.	**un panino.** *oon pahneenoh*
It's to go.	**È da portare via.** *eh dah pohrtahreh vee-ah*
That's all, thanks.	**È tutto, grazie.** *eh toot-toh grahtzee-eh*

table manners

Go ahead, treat yourself. You deserve a meal at a swanky restaurant!

A table for two, please.	**Un tavolo per due, per piacere.** *oon tahvohloh pehr doo-eh pehr pee-ahchehreh* *On a date, huh?*
We have a reservation.	**Abbiamo una prenotazione.** *ahb-bee-ahmoh oonah prehnoh-tahtzee-ohneh* *It's always good to think ahead.*
Could we sit …?	**Possiamo sederci …?** *pohs-see-ahmoh sehdehrchee* *Find a cozy, romantic spot.*
over there	**là** *lah*
outside	**fuori** *foo-ohree*
in a non-smoking area	**in una zona per non fumatori** *een oonah dzohnah pehr nohn foomah-tohree*
by the window	**vicino alla finestra** *veecheenoh ahl-lah feenehstrah*
Excuse me!	**Scusi!** *skoozee* *Say this to get the attention of the wait staff.*
Do you have a set menu?	**Avete un menù a prezzo fisso?** *ahvehteh oon mehnoo ah prehtzoh fees-soh*

Can you recommend some typical local dishes?	**Può consigliare dei piatti tipici della regione?**
	poo-oh kohnsee-lyahreh day pee-aht-tee teepeechee dehl-lah rehjohneh
	Want some local flavor, huh?!
What is …?	**Cos'è …?**
	kohzeh
	Avoid the shock when your meal arrives.
No … please!	**Senza … per piacere!**
	sehntzah … pehr pee-ahchehreh
	Check the dictionary in the back to fill in the blank.
Could I have …?	**Mi può portare …?**
	me poo-oh pohrtahreh
a fork	**una forchetta**
	oonah fohrkeht-tah
a glass	**un bicchiere**
	oon beek-keyehreh
a knife	**un coltello**
	oon kohltehl-loh
a napkin	**un tovagliolo**
	oon tohvah-lyohloh
a plate	**un piatto**
	oon pee-aht-toh
a spoon	**un cucchiaio**
	oon kook-key-ahee-oh
Where is the bathroom?	**Dov'è la toilette?**
	dohveh lah twah-leht
	Good question.

I can't eat food containing …	**Non posso mangiare piatti che contengono …**
	nohn pohs-soh mahnjahreh pee-aht-tee keh kohntehn-gohnoh
	Allergic to something? Make sure you explain.
Do you have vegetarian meals?	**Avete piatti vegetariani?**
	ahvehteh pee-aht-tee vehjeh-tahree-ahnee

Italians know how to eat well. Fast food joints offer goodies such as: "pizza"; "piadina", stuffed pizza; "gnocchi", potato dumplings; "tigella", rice croquettes; and other kinds of "stuzzicherie", snacks. Even though you can eat pretty well at an Italian fast food stand, going out for a sit-down meal at a nice restaurant is very popular—there's often live music to enjoy along with great wine and cocktails.

complaints

Go ahead and make a big stink.

That's not what I ordered.	**Non ho ordinato questo.**
	nohn oh orhdee-nahtoh kwehstoh
I asked for …	**Ho ordinato …**
	oh orhdee-nahtoh
This is cold.	**Questo è freddo.**
	kwehstoh eh frehd-doh

This isn't fresh. | **Questo non è fresco.**
kwehstoh nohn eh frehskoh

This isn't clean. | **Questo non è pulito.**
kwehstoh nohn eh pooleetoh

Don't put up with a nasty waiter.

– Scusi! Quanto dobbiamo aspettare ancora?
skoozee kwahntoh dohb-bee-ahmoh ahspeht-tahreh ahnkohrah
Excuse me! How much longer will our food be?

– Non lo so.
nohn loh soh
I don't know.

– Non possiamo più aspettare.
nohn pohs-see-ahmoh pew ahspeht-tahreh
We can't wait any longer.

good or gross?

Give the chef a compliment…

It's … | **È …**
eh

delicious. | **delizioso.**
dehleetzee-ohzoh

so good. | **buonissimo.**
bwohnees-seemoh

exquisite. | **squisito.**
skweezeetoh

45

Or not …

It's gross!	**Che schifo!** 🌡️
	keh skeefoh
It tastes disgusting.	**Ha un saporaccio.**
	ah oon sahpohrah-tchoh
What shit!	**Che merda!** 🌡️
	keh mehrdah

pay up

How much did that meal set you back?

The check, please.	**Il conto, per piacere.**
	eel kohntoh pehr pee-ahchehreh
We'd like to pay separately.	**Vorremmo pagare separatamente.**
	vohr-rehm-moh pahgahreh sehpah-rah-tah-mehnteh
	Goin' Dutch?
It's all together, please.	**Un conto unico, per piacere.**
	oon kohntoh ooneekoh pehr pee-ahchehreh
I think there's a mistake.	**Penso ci sia un errore.**
	pehnsoh chee see-ah oon ehr-rohreh
What is this amount for?	**Per cosa è questa cifra?**
	pehr kohzah eh kwehstah cheefrah
	If a café has both a counter and tables, there's usually a cover charge, "coperto", for table service. Ask about extra charges before you sit down. If resting your legs isn't worth the extra cash, eat your food at the bar or get it to go.

I didn't have that. I had …	**Non ho ordinato questo.**
	Ho ordinato …
	nohn oh orhdee-nahtoh kwehstoh
	oh orhdee-nahtoh

Is service included?	**Il servizio è compreso?**
	eel sehrveetzee-oh eh kohmprehzoh
	Service is usually included in the
	bill at most restaurants in Italy.
	Feel free to leave an extra 5–10%
	if the service is really great (or if
	your waiter is a hottie).

How much do you tip?	**Quant'è la mancia?**
	kwahnteh lah mahnchah
	If you're not sure, ask a cute
	local for some tips!

I'll pay with a credit card.	**Vorrei pagare con carta di credito.**
	vohr-ray pahgahreh kohn kahrtah dee
	krehdeetoh

I don't have enough cash.	**Non ho abbastanza contanti.**
	nohn oh ahb-bahstahntzah kohntahntee
	Pretty embarrassing…

| I'd like a receipt. | **Vorrei la ricevuta.** |
| | *vohr-ray lah reecheh-vootah* |

breakfast

Whether you have it early or late, ask for…

| I'd like … | **Vorrei …** |
| | *vohr-ray* |

| butter. | **del burro.** |
| | *dehl boor-roh* |

I'd like …	**Vorrei …**
	vohr-<u>ray</u>
coffee.	**un caffè.**
	oon kahf-<u>feh</u>
eggs.	**delle uova.**
	<u>dehl</u>-leh oo-<u>oh</u>vah
fried eggs.	**delle uova fritte.**
	<u>dehl</u>-leh oo-<u>oh</u>vah fr<u>eet</u>-teh
scrambled eggs.	**delle uova strapazzate.**
	<u>dehl</u>-leh oo-<u>oh</u>vah strahpah-<u>tzah</u>teh
honey.	**del miele.**
	dehl me-<u>ehl</u>eh
jam.	**della marmellata.**
	<u>dehl</u>-lah mahrmehl-<u>lah</u>tah
juice.	**un succo di frutta.**
	oon <u>sook</u>-koh dee <u>froot</u>-tah
grapefruit juice.	**un succo di pompelmo.**
	oon <u>sook</u>-koh dee pohmp<u>ehl</u>moh
orange juice.	**un succo d'arancia.**
	oon <u>sook</u>-koh dah<u>rahn</u>chah
marmalade.	**della composta di agrumi.**
	<u>dehl</u>-lah kohmp<u>oh</u>stah dee ah<u>groo</u>mee
milk.	**del latte.**
	dehl <u>laht</u>-teh
rolls.	**dei panini.**
	day pah<u>nee</u>nee
tea.	**un tè.**
	oon teh
toast.	**del pane tostato.**
	dehl <u>pah</u>neh toh<u>stah</u>toh

FACT

Think Italian food is just pizza and pasta? Think again. You will be amazed at the variety of food available throughout Italy: tasty hors d'œuvres, soups, traditional meat dishes, fresh fish, poultry, cheese, not to mention delicious and decadent cakes and "gelato", the famous Italian ice cream.

Ingredients and dishes vary greatly from north to south, and each region has its own specialty. The south is warm and sunny, and you'll find more pasta, fresh veggies, olive oil, and fish. In the colder, heartier north, dishes are often made with butter rather than olive oil. Flat or stuffed pasta, risotto, polenta, and a huge variety of meat are also common in the north.

soup

An Italian dinner includes a first course of soup or pasta, usually hearty enough to be a meal on its own. Try some of these favorites.

busecca
boozehk-kah
thick tripe, vegetable, and bean soup

cacciucco
kahtchook-koh
spicy seafood chowder

minestrone
meeneh-strohneh
vegetable and bean soup, sometimes served with noodles or cheese

stracciatella
strah-tchahtehl-lah
Roman egg-drop soup served with cheese

zuppa di fagioli
dzoop-pah dee fahjohlee
bean soup

zuppa di vongole
dzoop-pah dee vohngohleh
clam soup, with a base of white wine or tomatoes

FACT To Italians, all soup is not created equal; therefore, each variety has its own name. The most common word for soup, "zuppa", usually describes a thick soup with bread, meat, or fish. "Minestra", "minestrone", or "minestrina" is a soup with pasta, rice, vegetables, or beans. "Minestrone" is also the word for a specific vegetable and bean soup well-known even outside of Italy. Don't get overwhelmed! If you see something you don't recognize, just ask:

What's in this?   **Cosa c'è qua dentro?**
                    kohzah cheh kwah dehntroh

pasta

The infamous Italian first course…

fettuccine
feht-tootcheeneh
flat noodles made with eggs

orecchiette
ohrehk-keyeht-teh
literally, "little ears", this delicious pasta is shaped like 'em

penne
pehn-neh
tube-shaped pasta with diagonally cut ends

spaghetti
spahgh<u>eh</u>t-tee
long, thin noodles

tortellini
tohrtehl-<u>lee</u>nee
small dumplings stuffed with meat or cheese, seved in broth or sauce

Your pasta may be topped with one of these sauces.

al pomodoro
ahl pohmoh-<u>doh</u>roh
mixture of cooked tomatoes, garlic, and basil

bolognese
bohloh-<u>nyeh</u>zeh
Bologna's hearty sauce made with ground beef and sometimes "pancetta", ham

pesto
<u>peh</u>stoh
sauce made from basil, olive oil, and plenty of garlic

pizza

Once you've tried genuine pizza, you'll know why it's Italy's most famous food.

margherita
mahrghe-<u>ree</u>tah
the pizza ingredients (tomato, cheese, and basil or oregano) reflect Italy's national colors; try it in Naples, the birthplace of the modern pizza

napoletana
nahpohleh-<u>tah</u>nah
the classic pizza with anchovies, tomatoes, and cheese

quattro formaggi
kwaht-troh fohrmahdjee
cheese lovers' pizza with four types of cheese

quattro stagioni
kwaht-troh stahjohnee
"four seasons", with a variety of vegetables—tomatoes, artichokes, mushrooms, olives—plus cheese and ham

Pizza joints have always been a popular place to hang out but, in Italy, they can also be nighttime hotspots. Because pizzerias in Italy feature well-stocked bars in addition to delicious pizza, Italian hipsters will often spend their nights there, lounging over good food and great wine.

fish

You can find terrific fish in northern or southern Italy, and of course, on the Italian islands. If you're feeling adventurous, try…

anguilla alla veneziana
ahngweel-lah ahl-lah vehneh-tzee-ahnah
eel cooked in sauce made from tuna and lemon

lumache alla milanese
loomahkeh ahl-lah meelah-nehzeh
snails with anchovy, fennel, and wine sauce

Or stick with your favorites…

cod	**merluzzo** *mehrlootzoh*
crab	**granchio** *grahnkey-oh*
octopus	**polpo** *pohlpoh*
salmon	**salmone** *sahlmohneh*
shrimp	**gamberi** *gahm-behree*
sole	**sogliola** *sohlyohlah*
swordfish	**pesce spada** *pehsheh spahdah*
trout	**trota** *trohtah*
tuna	**tonno** *tohn-noh*

you carnivore

If it's meat you want, you can find plenty of it in Italy. Here are some of the classics.

bistecca alla fiorentina
beestehk-kah ahl-lah fee-ohrehn-teenah
grilled steak flavored with pepper, lemon juice, and parsley;
a favorite in Florence

cotoletta alla milanese

kohtoh<u>leht</u>-tah <u>ahl</u>-lah meelah-<u>neh</u>zeh

breaded veal cutlet

involtini

eenvohl-<u>tee</u>nee

thin slices of meat rolled and stuffed with ham

polenta e coniglio

poh<u>lehn</u>tah eh koh<u>nee</u>-lyoh

rabbit stew with cornmeal paste

pollo alla romana

<u>pohl</u>-loh <u>ahl</u>-lah roh<u>mah</u>nah

diced chicken with tomato sauce and sweet peppers

saltimbocca alla romana

sahlteem-<u>bohk</u>-kah <u>ahl</u>-lah roh<u>mah</u>nah

veal cutlet braised in marsala wine with ham and sage

Not sure what to order? Just order the basics.

beef	**manzo**
	<u>mahn</u>dzoh
chicken	**pollo**
	<u>pohl</u>-loh
ham	**prosciutto**
	proh<u>shoot</u>-toh
lamb	**agnello**
	ahny<u>ehl</u>-loh
pork	**maiale**
	mahee-<u>ahl</u>eh
veal	**vitello**
	vee<u>tehl</u>-loh

herbivore

Think greens are just for salads? Check out these favorite Italian veggie dishes but make sure to save room for dessert.

carciofi alla giudea
kahrchoh-fee ahl-lah jewdeh-ah
deep-fried artichoke, originally a specialty of Rome's old Jewish quarter

funghi porcini arrosto
foonghee pohrcheenee ahr-rohstoh
mushrooms roasted or grilled with garlic, parsley, and chili peppers

peperoni ripieni
pehpeh-rohnee reepee-ehnee
stuffed sweet peppers usually with ground meat; also try "zucchini ripieni", stuffed zucchini

Or sample any of these…

cabbage	**cavolo** *kahvohloh*
cherries	**ciliege** *cheelee-ehjeh*
grapes	**uva** *oovah*
lettuce	**lattuga** *laht-toogah*
mushrooms	**funghi** *foonghee*
onions	**cipolle** *cheepohl-leh*

orange	**arancia** *ah<u>rahn</u>chah*
peach	**pesca** *<u>peh</u>skah*
peas	**piselli** *pee<u>zehl</u>-lee*
raspberries	**lamponi** *lahm<u>poh</u>nee*
strawberries	**fragole** *<u>frah</u>gohleh*
tomato	**pomodoro** *pohmoh-<u>doh</u>roh*
watermelon	**anguria** NORTHERN ITALY **cocomero** SOUTHERN ITALY *ahn<u>goo</u>ree-ah / koh<u>koh</u>-mehroh*

FACT You already know more Italian than you think! You won't need to reach for your dictionary when you see "asparagi", "broccoli", "carote", "patate", "spinaci", or "zucchini" on the menu. You'll probably also recognize some common Italian fruit: "banane", "limone", "melone", and "pera". Don't be fooled by "prugna" though—it means plum.

cheese please

Italy has an amazing selection of local cheese. You may already know and love some of these, but be sure to sample…

gorgonzola
gohrgohn-<u>dzoh</u>lah
blue-veined cheese with a tangy flavor

mozzarella
mohtzah<u>rehl</u>-lah
soft, unripened cheese made from buffalo's milk in the south, elsewhere with cow's milk

parmigiano
pahrmee-<u>jah</u>noh
parmesan, a hard cheese generally grated ("-reggiano") for use in hot dishes and pasta but also eaten alone

pecorino
pehkoh-<u>reen</u>oh
strongly-flavored sheep's milk cheese—say someone smells like "pecorino" and you've insulted him/her…

provolone
prohvoh-<u>loh</u>neh
a firm, tasty cheese

ricotta
ree<u>koht</u>-tah
soft cow's or sheep's milk cheese

dessert

Hope you saved room!

biscotti
bees<u>koht</u>-tee
crunchy twice-baked cookies—try dippin' 'em in coffee or sweet wine

cannoli
kahn-<u>noh</u>lee
a fried pastry shell filled with cream made from ricotta cheese

gelato
jeh<u>lah</u>toh
Italian ice cream is not to be missed; try: "fiordilatte", cream flavored; "caffè", coffee; "frutti di bosco", wild berry; "stracciatella", chocolate chip.

tiramisù
teerah-mee<u>soo</u>
a layered treat made from mascarpone, eggs, coffee, and sponge cake

panettone
pahneht-<u>toh</u>neh
cake made with fruit and nuts

overeating

Did you just pig out?

God, what a feast!	**Madonna, che abbuffata!** 🌡 *mah<u>dohn</u>-nah keh ahb-boof-<u>fah</u>tah*
I ate like a pig.	**Ho mangiato come un bue.** *oh mahn<u>jah</u>toh <u>koh</u>meh oon boo-eh* *Literally: I ate like an ox.*
It's gross how much I ate!	**Ho mangiato da fare schifo!** *oh mahn<u>jah</u>toh dah <u>fah</u>reh <u>skee</u>foh*
I'm full.	**Sono pieno come un uovo.** *<u>soh</u>noh pee-<u>eh</u>noh <u>koh</u>meh oon oo-<u>oh</u>voh* *Literally: I'm full like an egg.*

And now?

I feel like …	**Mi viene da …** *me vee-<u>eh</u>neh dah*
throwing up.	**rimettere.** *ree<u>meht</u>-tehreh*
vomiting.	**vomitare.** *vohmee-<u>tah</u>reh*
puking.	**dare di stomaco.** *<u>dah</u>reh dee <u>stoh</u>mahkoh*

DRINKS

what to drink

When you need to detox, ask for...

I'd like ...	**Vorrei ...**
	vohr-ray
a coffee.	**un caffè.**
	oon kahf-feh
a tea.	**un tè.**
	oon teh
a hot chocolate.	**una cioccolata calda.**
	oonah chohk-kohlahtah kahldah
a mineral water.	**dell'acqua minerale.**
	dehl-lahk-kwah meeneh-rahleh
carbonated / non-carbonated	**gassata / naturale**
	gahs-sahtah / nahtoo-rahleh
a lemonade.	**una limonata.**
	oonah leemoh-nahtah

the
scoop

If you ask for "un caffè" you'll usually be served an espresso—strong, dark, and packed with caffeine. You can get your caffè "con panna" (with cream) or "con latte" (with milk). If you just want a small amount of milk, ask for a "caffè macchiato". "Un cappuccino" (coffee and hot milk, sometimes dusted with cocoa) is a must; in summer, un "caffè freddo" (iced coffee) is popular. If all this strong coffee isn't for you, you can ask for a "caffè lungo" or a "caffè americano", espresso diluted with hot water.

beer

Ready for a buzz?

Do you have … beer? | **Avete della birra …?**
ahvehteh dehl-lah beer-rah

bottled | **in bottiglia**
een boht-tee-lyah

draft | **alla spina**
ahl-lah speenah

shots!

To drink like a local, try an "aperitivo" before a meal and a "digestivo" after.

Aperitivi

Campari®
kahmpahree
reddish-brown bitters with orange peel and herbs

Martini® / Cinzano®
mahrteenee / cheen-tzahnoh
these two brands of vermouth are available sweet or dry

Digestivi

limoncello
leemohn-chehl-loh
a lemon-flavored liquor served as a shot—straight from the freezer—or over desserts and, sometimes, in mixed drinks

sambuca
sahm-bookah
a strong, anise-flavored drink: if you like the flavor but need something a little milder, try "anisette"

Before- and after-dinner drinks are great, but what should you drink to look cool when you hit the bars? Try a "Negroni®" (gin, red vermouth, and bitter "Campari®"), a "mojito" (white rum, club soda, brown sugar, and mint leaves), or a "caipiroska" (vodka, lime, sugar).

FACT

Tipping in bars in Italy is very rare. If you're in a generous mood or want to get the attention of a hot bartender, you can add a euro onto your tab.

wine

Go ahead and order a glass—or bottle—of the best.

I'd like ... of red wine / white wine.	**Vorrei ... di *vino bianco / vino rosso.*** vohr-<u>ray</u> ... dee <u>vee</u>-noh bee-<u>ahn</u>koh / <u>vee</u>-<u>noh</u> <u>rohs</u>-soh
a carafe	**una caraffa** <u>oo</u>nah kah<u>rahf</u>-fah
a bottle	**una bottiglia** <u>oo</u>nah boht-<u>tee</u>-lyah
a glass	**un bicchiere** oon beek-key<u>eh</u>reh
I'd like the house wine, please.	**Desidero il vino della casa, per favore.** deh<u>zee</u>-dehroh eel <u>vee</u>-noh <u>dehl</u>-lah kah<u>zah</u> pehr fah<u>voh</u>reh

yo!

Having trouble remembering all those Italian wines?
Start by reading the label.

semi-dry	**abboccato** *ahb-bohk-<u>kah</u>toh*
slightly sweet	**amabile** *ah<u>mah</u>-beeleh*
guarantee of origin	**DOC** *dohk*
highest quality wine	**DOCG** *dohk-<u>jee</u>*
sweet	**dolce** *<u>dohl</u>-cheh*
light	**leggero** *leh-<u>djeh</u>roh*
full-bodied	**corposo** *kohr<u>poh</u>zoh*
rosé	**rosato / rosatello** *roh<u>zah</u>to / rohzah<u>tehl</u>-loh*
dry	**secco** *<u>sehk</u>-koh*
sparkling	**frizzante** *free-dz<u>ah</u>nteh*
local wine	**vino del paese** *<u>vee</u>-noh dehl pah<u>eh</u>zeh*

bottoms up

Ready to get smashed?

Should we go …?	**Andiamo a …?** *ahndee-ahmoh ah*
have a stiff drink	**farci l'ammazzacaffè** *fahrchee lahm-mahtzah-kahf-feh* *Literally: take a coffee killer*
have a glass	**farci un bicchiere** *fahrchee oon beek-keyehreh*
drink a drop	**bere un goccio** *behreh oon goh-tchoh*
for a beer	**farci una birra** *fahrchee oonah beer-rah*
drink down a bottle of wine	**scolarci una boccia di vino** *skoh-lahrchee oonah boh-tchah dee vee-noh* *"Scolarci", comes from the verb "scolarsi", to drain.*
have a shot	**farci un cicchettino** *fahrchee oon cheek-keht-teenoh*

cheers

Before you drink, make a toast.

Cheers!	**Cin cin!** *cheen cheen*
To health!	**Salute!** *sahlooteh*
To our (health)!	**Alla nostra!** *ahl-lah nohstrah*

| To the drop! | **Alla goccia!** |
| | *ahl-lah goh-tchah* |

drunk

Did you, or someone else, have a little too much to drink? Here's how to talk about it.

Maria is a heavy drinker.	**Maria beve come una spugna.**
	maree-ah behveh kohmeh oonah spoonyah
	Literally: Maria drinks like a sponge.

I drank a lot.	**Ho bevuto un casino.**
	oh behvootoh oon kahzeenoh
	"Casino" is a word that means many things: brothel, mess—but as an adverb, like in this case, it means a lot.

| I drank so much, it's gross! | **Ho bevuto da fare schifo!** |
| | *oh behvootoh dah fahreh skeefoh* |

Suffer the consequences...

– **Guarda un po'! Elena è già fuori!**
gwahrdah oon poh ehlehnah eh jah foo-ohree
Look! Elena is already drunk!

– **Come? Di già?**
kohmeh dee jah
What? Already?

yo! Italians have many ways to say that someone's drunk.

Francesco <u>is drunk</u>.

Francesco ...
frahn-<u>cheh</u>skoh

è ubriaco duro / fradicio.
eh oobree-<u>ah</u>koh <u>doo</u>roh / <u>frah</u>deechoh
Literally: is a hard / soaked drunk

è bresco. BOLOGNA
eh <u>breh</u>skoh

si è preso una gran ciucca.
see eh <u>preh</u>zoh <u>oo</u>nah grahn <u>chook</u>-kah
Literally: took a great drink

è fuori come un balcone.
eh foo-<u>ohre</u> <u>koh</u>meh oon bahl<u>koh</u>neh
Literally: is out like a balcony

è fuori come un culo.
eh foo-<u>ohre</u> <u>koh</u>meh oon <u>koo</u>loh
Literally: is out like an ass

è ciucco.
eh <u>chook</u>-koh

hangover

Drank too much? Not feeling too well? Share your discomfort.

I have a big hangover.

Ho una gran cassa. BOLOGNA
oh <u>oo</u>nah grahn <u>kahs</u>-sah
Literally: I have a big case.

My head is spinning.

Ho un gran cerchio alla testa.
oh oon grahn <u>chehr</u>-key-oh <u>ahl</u>-lah <u>teh</u>stah
Literally: I have a big circle around my head.

7 HAVIN' FUN

beach bum

Grab your shades and get some sun.

Where's the beach?	**Dov'è la spiaggia?** *dohveh lah spee-ahdjah*
Is it a nude beach?	**È una spiaggia per nudisti?** *eh oonah spee-ahdjah pehr noodeestee*
Is there a swimming pool?	**C'è una piscina?** *cheh oonah peeshee-nah*
Is there a lifeguard?	**C'è un bagnino?** *cheh oon bahnyeenoh* *What you really wanna know:* *Is the lifeguard hot?!*
I want to rent …	**Vorrei noleggiare …** *vohr-ray nohleh-djahreh*
a deck chair.	**una sedia a sdraio.** *oonah sehdee-ah ah zdrahee-oh*
diving equipment.	**attrezzature da sub.** *aht-trehtzahtooreh dah soob*
a jet-ski.	**una moto d'acqua.** *oonah mohtoh dahk-kwah*
a motorboat.	**una barca a motore.** *oonah bahrkah ah mohtohreh*
a surfboard.	**una tavola da surf.** *oonah tahvohlah dah sehrf*
an umbrella.	**un ombrellone.** *oon ohmbrehl-lohneh*
water skis.	**degli sci d'acqua.** *deh-lyee shee dahk-kwah*

the scoop

With close to 5,000 miles of coastline, you're bound to end up at the beach while in Italy! Favorite areas for sunning are Liguria, Tuscany's seaside, and the Adriatic and Amalfi coasts. Be sure to visit the islands surrounding Italy—Sicily and Sardinia for example—they also have a lot of sun and sand!

party time

Italians know how to have a good time.

What's there to do at night?	**Cosa si può fare la sera?** *kohzah see poo-oh fahreh lah sehrah*
Let's go dancing!	**Andiamo a ballare!** *ahndee-ahmoh ah bahl-lahreh*
Let's go drink something.	**Andiamo a bere qualcosa.** *ahndee-ahmoh ah behreh kwahl-kohzah*
Do you know …?	**Conosci …?** *kohnoh-shee*
a nice bar	**un bar carino** *oon bahr kahreenoh*
a hot spot	**un locale vivace** *oon lohkahleh veevahcheh*
a good club	**un bel disco pub** *oon behl deeskoh pahb*
What type of music do they play?	**Che tipo di musica suonano?** *keh teepoh dee moozeekah swohnahnoh*

69

| Is there … in town? | **C'è … in città?** |
| | *cheh … een cheet-tah* |

| a gay club | **un locale gay** |
| | *oon loh<u>kah</u>leh gay* |

| a nightclub | **un night (club)** |
| | *oon night (club)* |

Wanna have some fun?

– Ti va di uscire stasera?
tee vah dee oo<u>shee</u>-reh stah-<u>seh</u>rah
Do you want to go out tonight?
_____

– Sì! Andiamo a ballare?
see ahndee-<u>ah</u>moh ah bahl-<u>lah</u>reh
Yeah! Wanna go dancing?
_____

– Certo!
<u>chehr</u>toh
Sure!

Like to party? Italians start partying when they're pretty young. They hang out at local hot spots in town when they're 12 or 13 years old. At around 16, they pass the time away in dance clubs and pizzerias. Many of these clubs and pizzerias serve alcohol and, though the drinking age is officially 18, few places respect the rule.

smoke

Whether you'd like to light up or want to share your distaste of smoking with those around you, here's the language you need.

Do you have <u>a cigarette</u>?

Hai …?
ahee

una sigaretta
<u>oo</u>nah seegah<u>reht</u>-tah
The standard.

una siga
<u>oo</u>nah <u>see</u>gah
Used by young smokers.

una paglia
<u>oo</u>nah <u>pah</u>lyah
Literally: a straw
This one can also mean marijuana.

da fumare
dah foo<u>mah</u>reh
Literally: a smoke

Do you mind if I smoke?	**Ti dà fastidio se fumo?** *tee dah fah<u>steed</u>ee-oh seh <u>foo</u>moh*
You're such a chain smoker.	**Te ne stai accendendo una dopo l'altra.** *teh neh <u>stah</u>-ee ah-tchehn-<u>dehn</u>doh <u>oo</u>nah <u>doh</u>poh <u>lahl</u>trah*
Stop smoking!	**Smettila di fumare!** *<u>zmeht</u>-teelah dee foo<u>mah</u>reh*
Can I have a drag?	**Mi fai dare due tiri?** *me <u>fah</u>-ee <u>dah</u>reh <u>doo</u>-eh <u>tee</u>ree*

71

spa

You need a complete detox!

I'd like …	**Vorrei …** *vohr-ray*
a facial.	**un massaggio facciale.** *oon mahs-sah-djoh fah-tchahleh*
a face cleansing.	**una pulizia del viso.** *oonah poolee-tzee-ah dehl veezoh*
a relaxing massage.	**un massaggio rilassante.** *oon mahs-sah-djoh reelahs-sahnteh*
a manicure.	**farmi le unghie.** *fahr-mee leh oonghee-eh*
a pedicure.	**un pedicure.** *oon pehdee-kewr*
an eyebrow wax.	**farmi le sopracciglia.** *fahr-mee leh sohprah-tcheelyaha*
a bikini wax.	**una ceretta nella zona bikini.** *oonah chehreht-tah nehl-lah dzohnah beekeenee*

Italy is famous for its "beauty-farms", places to go for skin care, treatments, massage, and general relaxation. Some are day-spas and others are hotel spas, where guests can be pampered all weekend—if not longer!

body alterations

Blend in with the locals.

I had …

Mi sono rifatta …
me sohnoh reefaht-tah
Literally: I remade

a boob job.

il seno.
eel sehnoh

a nose job.

il naso.
eel nahzoh

my chin done.

il doppio mento.
eel dohp-pee-oh mehntoh
Literally: a double chin removed

She enhanced her …

Si è siliconata …
see eh seelee-kohnahtah

boobs.

le tette.
leh teht-teh

lips.

le labbra.
leh lahb-brah

butt.

le chiappe.
leh key-ahp-peh

She is totally re-made!

È completamente rifatta!
eh kohmpleh-tahmehnteh reefaht-tah

He has … piercing.

Ha il piercing …
ah eel piercing

a belly button

all'ombelico.
ahl-lohmbeh-leekoh

an eyebrow

al sopracciglio.
ahl sohprah-tcheelyoh

73

He has … piercing.	**Ha il piercing …**
	ah eel piercing
a nipple	**sul capezzolo.**
	sool kahpeh-tzohloh
a nose	**al naso.**
	ahl nahzoh
a genital	**lì.**
	lee
	Literally: there. Ouch!
He has a cool tattoo.	**Ha un tatuaggio troppo figo.**
	ah oon tahtoo-ahdjoh trohp-poh feegoh

the sights

See and be seen.

How much does the tour cost?	**Quanto costa il giro?**
	kwahntoh kohstah eel jeeroh
Can we stop here …?	**Possiamo fermarci qui …?**
	pohs-see-ahmoh fehrmahrchee kwee
to take photographs	**per fare fotografie**
	pehr fahreh fohtoh-grahfee-eh
to buy souvenirs	**per comprare dei souvenir**
	pehr kohmprahreh day soovehneer
to go to the bathroom	**per andare alla toilette**
	pehr ahndahreh ahl-lah twah-leht
Would you take a photo of us?	**Le dispiace farci una fotografia?**
	leh deespee-ahcheh fahrchee oonah fohtoh-grahfee-ah
	Capture the memory, but keep an eye on your camera.

| Where's the …? | **Dov'è …?** |
| | *dohveh* |

art gallery	**la galleria d'arte**
	lah gahl-lehree-ah dahrteh
botanical garden	**il giardino botanico**
	eel jahrdeenoh bohtah-neekoh
castle	**il castello**
	eel kahstehl-loh
cemetery	**il cimitero**
	eel cheemee-tehroh
church	**la chiesa**
	lah key-ehzah
downtown area	**il centro**
	eel chehntroh
lake	**il lago**
	eel lahgoh
market	**il mercato**
	eel mehrkahtoh
museum	**il museo**
	eel moozeh-oh
nature preserve	**l'oasi naturale**
	loh-ahzee nahtoo-rahleh
old town	**la città vecchia**
	lah cheet-tah vehk-keyah
palace	**il palazzo**
	eel pahlahtzoh
park	**il parco**
	eel pahrkoh
vineyard/winery	**il vigneto**
	eel veenyehtoh

| What are the hours? | **Qual è l'orario di apertura?** |
| | *kwahleh lohrahree-oh dee ahpehr-toorah* |

75

Can I take photos?	**Posso fare fotografie?**
	pohs-soh _fahreh fohtoh-grahfee-eh_
How much is the entrance fee?	**Quant'è il biglietto d'ingresso?**
	kwahnteh eel bee-lyeht-toh deengrehs-soh
Are there any discounts for students?	**Ci sono riduzioni per studenti?**
	chee sohnoh reedootzee-ohnee pehr
	stew-dehntee

| **yo!** | Don't hold back—share your impressions. |

| It's … | **È …** |
| | _eh_ |

beautiful.	**bello♂ / bella♀.**
	behl-loh / behl-lah
boring.	**noioso♂ / noiosa♀.**
	noh-ee-ohzoh / noh-ee-ohzah
cool.	**troppo figo.**
	trohp-poh feegoh
great.	**della Madonna*.**
	dehl-lah mahdohn-nah
romantic.	**romantico♂ / romantica♀.**
	rohmahn-teekoh / rohmahn-teekah
shitty.	**di merda.**
	dee mehrdah
strange.	**strano♂ / strana♀.**
	strahnoh / strahnah
ugly.	**brutto♂ / brutta♀.**
	broot-toh / broot-tah

* Use "della Madonna" (literally: of the Madonna) to describe something or
  someone—and bring it, him, or her to a higher level…

entertainment

In the mood for a little culture?

Do you have a program of events?	**Avete un programma delle manifestazioni?**
	ah_veh_teh oon prohg_rahm_-mah _dehl_-leh mahnee-fehstah-tzee_eohnee_
	Large and small towns often have guides with listings of local events; be sure to check 'em out!
Can you recommend …?	**Può consigliare …?**
	poo-_oh_ kohnsee-_lyah_reh
a concert	**un concerto**
	oon kohn_chehr_toh
a movie	**un film**
	oon feelm
What time does it start?	**A che ora comincia?**
	ah keh _oh_rah koh_meen_-chah
Where can I get tickets?	**Dove si comprano i biglietti?**
	_doh_veh see _kohm_prahnoh ee bee-_lyeht_-tee
How much is the ticket?	**Quanto costa il biglietto?**
	_kwahn_toh _koh_stah eel bee-_lyeht_-toh
Do you have anything cheaper?	**Ha qualcosa di meno caro?**
	ah kwahl-_koh_zah dee _meh_noh _kah_roh
Is there a movie theater nearby?	**C'è un cinema qui vicino?**
	cheh oon _chee_nehmah kwee vee_chee_noh
Is the film *dubbed / subtitled*?	**Il film *è doppiato / ha i sottotitoli*?**
	eel feelm eh dohp-pee-_ah_toh /ah ee soht-toht_tee_-tohlee

music

Get into the groove—in Italian.

I love ...	**Mi piace ...** *me pee-ahcheh*
pop music.	**la musica pop.** *lah moozeekah pohp*
Italian rock.	**il rock italiano.** *eel rohk eetahlee-ahnoh*
the music of the 60s/ 70s / 80s.	**la musica anni '60 / '70 / '80.** *lah moozeekah ahn-nee sehs-sahntah / seht-tahntah / oht-tahntah*
hip-hop.	**l'hip-hop.** *lee-poh*

yo!

Can't live without your tunes? Make sure you have these.

CD player	**il lettore (di) CD** *eel teht-tohreh (dee) chee dee*
discman	**discman** *deeskmahn*
headphones	**le cuffie** *leh koof-fee-eh*
MP3 player	**il lettore (di) MP3** *eel teht-tohreh (dee) ehm-meh pee treh*
radio	**la radio** *lah rahdee-oh*

sports

Get active.

Do you like …? | **Ti piace …?**
tee pee-ahcheh

baseball | **il baseball**
eel behs-bohl

basketball | **il basket**
eel bahskeht

boxing | **la box**
lah bohx

cycling | **il ciclismo**
eel cheeklee-zmoh

skateboarding | **lo skateboard**
loh skeht-bohrd

soccer | **il calcio**
eel kahl-choh

 Italy has tons of beaches and mountains. While you're there, why not get physical with the locals?

water skiing | **lo sci nautico**
loh she nahoo-teekoh

kitesurfing | **il kite-surf**
eel kaheet-surf

You'll have plenty of opportunities to try out this extreme variation on "il wind-surf", wind-surfing.

skiing | **lo sci**
loh shee

snowboarding | **lo snowboard**
loh znoh-bohrd

spectator sports

Prefer watching sports to actually playing them?

Is there a soccer game this Saturday?

C'è una partita di calcio il sabato?
cheh oonah pahrteetah dee kahl-choh eel sahbahtoh

Can you get me a ticket?

Può comprarmi un biglietto?
poo-oh kohmprahrme oon bee-lyeht-toh

What's the admission charge?

Quant'è il biglietto d'ingresso?
kwahnteh eel bee-lyeht-toh deengrehs-soh

FACT Italians are avid soccer fans, and will scream almost anything to motivate their team—they've even been known to personalize songs about their favorite team or players. A very popular song in Rome is "Ma che siete venuti a fa'?" *What did you come for?* What they really mean is: You came to lose!

soccer match

Show a little team spirit, in Italian!

Go for it!
Forza!
fohrtzah

Cheer up!
Alè alè!
ahleh ahleh

Go this way!
Vai così!
vah-ee kohzee

We are the champions.
Siamo solo noi.
see-ahmoh sohloh noh-ee
This refers to a famous song by
Vasco Rossi.

Make us dream!
Facci sognare!
fah-tchee sohnyahreh

score!

Share your excitement about the team's moves.

It was a/an … move!
È stata una partita …!
eh stahtah oonah pahrteetah

fantastic
fantastica
fahntah-steekah

amazing
mitica
meeteekah
Literally: mythical

out-of-this-world
da fine del mondo
dah feeneh dehl mohndoh

82

It was a ... goal.	**È stato un goal ...**
	eh <u>stah</u>toh oon gohl
wonderful	**della Madonna.**
	<u>dehl</u>-lah mah<u>dohn</u>-nah
	Literally: from the Madonna
spectacular	**spettacolare.**
	speht-tahkoh-<u>lah</u>reh
heavenly	**divino.**
	dee<u>vee</u>noh

insults

Your job as a spectator is to harass the referee and humiliate the opponents.

Ref, you're a bastard!	**Arbitro bastardo!** 🌡
	<u>ahr</u>beetroh bah<u>stahr</u>doh
Ref, you took a bribe!	**Arbitro venduto!** 🌡
	<u>ahr</u>beetroh vehn<u>doo</u>toh
Throw that @#&!ing ball!	**Tira quel cazzo di palla!** 🌡
	<u>tee</u>rah kwehl <u>kah</u>-tzoh dee <u>pahl</u>-lah
What a @#&!ing ref!	**Che arbitro del cazzo!** 🌡
	keh <u>ahr</u>beetroh dehl <u>kah</u>-tzoh
Son of a bitch!	**Figlio di puttana!** 🌡
	<u>fee</u>-lyoh dee poot-<u>tah</u>nah
Piece of shit!	**Pezzo di merda!** 🌡
	<u>peh</u>tzoh dee <u>mehr</u>dah
@#&! off!	**Vaffanculo!** 🌡
	vahf-fahn<u>koo</u>loh

You dick!	**Sei un coglione!** 
	say oon kohl<u>yoh</u>neh
What a @#&!-up!	**Che cappella!**
	keh kahp-<u>pehl</u>-lah

training

Don't let your body go just because you're on vacation.

Let's …	**Andiamo …**
	ahndee-<u>ah</u>moh
to the gym.	**in palestra.**
	een pahl<u>eh</u>strah
exercise.	**a fare un po' di movimento.**
	ah <u>fah</u>reh oon poh dee mohvee-<u>meh</u>ntoh
	Literally: move a little bit
do aerobics.	**ad aerobica.**
	ahdah-ehr<u>oh</u>beekah
lift weights.	**a far pesi.**
	ah fahr <u>peh</u>zee

ironman

What do you like to do at the gym?

| I go … | **Vado …** |
| | *vahdoh* |

spinning.
a fare spinning.
ah fahreh speen-neeng

to use the treadmill.
a fare un po' di tapis roulant.
ah fahreh oon poh dee tahpee roolahn

to use the fitness bike.
a fare un po' di cyclette.
ah fahreh oon poh dee chee-kleht

| Do you have …? | **Avete …?** |
| | *ahvehteh* |

a sauna
la sauna
lah sah-oonah

a steam room
il bagno turco
eel bahnyoh toorkoh

massage service
i massaggi
ee mahs-sahdjee

gambling

Got money to burn?

What did you bet on?
Su chi hai puntato?
soo key ahee poontahtoh

Did you place your bet?
Hai già puntato?
ahee jah poontahtoh

I bet 100 (euros) on …	**Ho puntato 100 sul …**
	oh poon<u>tah</u>toh <u>chehn</u>toh sool
They @#&!ed me!	**Mi hanno fottuto!**
	me <u>ahn</u>-noh foht-<u>too</u>toh
Luck is against me.	**Ho la sfiga che mi perseguita.**
	oh lah <u>sfee</u>gah keh me pehr<u>seh</u>-gweetah

 Italians have combined the best of two worlds: sports and gambling. "Totocalcio" is a national soccer lottery game; simply fill in the coupon with the teams you think will win. If you manage to get the goal of 14 points, you win a cash prize. A smaller prize is awarded to those who get 13 points. Another popular game is the virtual "Fantacalcio". You create your own team with current players and organize your own championships. The results are based on how your players perform during the real matches!

small talk

Get a polite conversation goin'.

My name is …	**Sono …** *sohnoh* *A simple way to introduce yourself.*
What's your name?	**Come si chiama?** *kohmeh see kee-ahmah*
Where are you from?	**Di dov'è?** *dee dohveh* *Always a good ice-breaker…*
Whom are you with?	**Con chi è?** *kohn key eh* *Find out if he or she is single before things go too far.*
I'm on my own.	**Sono da solo ♂ / sola ♀.** *sohnoh dah sohloh / sohlah*
I'm with …	**Sono con …** *sohnoh kohn*
a friend.	**amico ♂ / un'amica ♀.** *oon ahmeekoh / oonah-meekah*
my boyfriend / my girlfriend.	**il mio ragazzo ♂ / la mia ragazza ♀.** *eel me-oh rahgah-tzoh / lah me-ah rahgah-tzah*
my family.	**la mia famiglia.** *lah me-ah fahmeelyah*
my parents.	**i miei genitori.** *ee me-ay jehnee-tohree*

I'm with …

Vengo con …
vehngo kon

my father / my mother.

mio padre♂ / mia madre♀.
mee-oh pahdreh / me-ah mahdreh

my brother / my sister.

mio fratello♂ / mia sorella♀.
mee-oh frahtehl-loh / mee-ah sohrehl-lah

chitchat

These will help you keep his or her attention.

Che lavoro fa?

Lavoro per Berlitz.

What do you do?

Che lavoro fa?
keh lahvohroh fah
Find out some more about him or her.

What do you study?

Che cosa studia?
keh kohzah stew-dee-ah

Che cosa studia?

Studio scienze.

I'm studying …	**Studio …**
	stew-dee-oh
the arts.	**arte.**
	ahrteh
business.	**economia e commercio.**
	ehkoh-noh<u>mee</u>-ah eh kohm-<u>mehr</u>choh
science.	**scienze.**
	<u>shee</u>-ehn-tzeh
Whom do you work for?	**Per chi lavora?**
	pehr key lah<u>voh</u>rah
I work for …	**Lavoro per …**
	lah<u>voh</u>roh pehr
What are your _interests /_ _hobbies_?	**Quali sono i Suoi _interessi_ / _hobby_?**
	<u>kwah</u>lee <u>soh</u>noh ee soo-<u>oh</u>-ee eenteh<u>rehs</u>-see / <u>ohb</u>-bee
	Perhaps you have something in common.
I like …	**Mi piace …**
	me pee-<u>ah</u>cheh
music.	**la musica.**
	lah <u>moo</u>zeekah
reading.	**leggere.**
	<u>leh</u>-djehreh
sports.	**lo sport.**
	loh spohrt

makin' plans

Get together!

May I invite you to lunch?	**Posso invitarLa a pranzo?** *pohs-soh eenvee-tahrlah ah prahndzoh*
What are your plans for …?	**Cosa fa …?** *kohzah fah*
today	**oggi** *ohdjee*
tonight	**stasera** *stah-sehrah*
tomorrow	**domani** *dohmah-nee*
Are you free this eveing?	**È libero ♂ / libera ♀ stasera?** *eh leebehroh / leebehrah stah-sehrah*
Would you like to …?	**Le andrebbe di …?** *leh ahndrehb-beh dee*
go dancing	**andare a ballare** *ahndahreh ah bahl-lahreh*
go for a drink	**andare al bar** *ahndahreh ahl bahr*
go for a walk	**fare una passeggiata** *fahreh oonah pahs-sehdjahtah*
go shopping	**andare a fare acquisti** *ahndahreh ah fahreh ahk-kweestee*
I'd like to go to …	**Mi andrebbe di …** *me ahndrehb-beh dee*
What about a movie?	**Vuoi di andare al cinema?** *voo-ohee ahndahreh ahl cheenehmah*

91

How about another day?	**Facciamo un altro giorno?**
	fah-tchahmoh oon ahltroh johrnoh
	Do you really mean it, or are you just brushing someone off?

| Thanks, but I'm busy. | **Grazie, ma ho un altro impegno.** |
| | *grahtzee-eh mah oh oon ahltroh eempehnyoh* |

| Can I bring a friend? | **Posso portare un amico♂ / un'amica♀?** |
| | *pohs-soh pohrtahreh oon ahmeekoh / oon ahmeekah* |

| When should we meet? | **Quando ci incontriamo?** |
| | *kwahndoh chee eenkohntree-ahmoh* |

hangin' out

Get a little closer with these.

| Let me buy you a drink. | **Mi permetta di offrirLe una bibita.** |
| | *me pehrmeht-tah dee ohf-freerleh oonah beebee-tah* |

| What would you like? | **Cosa prende?** |
| | *kohzah prehndeh* |

| Why are you laughing? | **Perché ride?** |
| | *pehrkeh reedeh* |

Is my Italian that bad?	**Parlo così male l'italiano?**
	pahrloh kohzee mahleh leetahlee-ahnoh
	You know it's not, but it's always fun to be silly.

Wanna go somewhere quieter?	**Andiamo in un posto più tranquillo?** *ahndee-ahmoh een oon pohstoh pew trahnkweel-loh* *Such as...?*
Thanks for the evening.	**Grazie per la serata.** *grahtzee-eh pehr lah sehrahtah*
I'm afraid I have to leave.	**Penso che sia ora di andare.** *pehnsoh keh see-ah ohrah dee ahndahreh*
See you soon.	**A presto.** *ah prehstoh*
Can I have your address?	**Posso avere il Suo indirizzo?** *pohs-soh ahvehreh eel soo-oh eendee-reetzoh* *Ready for a long distance relationship?*

FACT There are formal and informal ways to say "you" in Italian. When you're talking to relatives, kids, and close friends (or lovers) use the informal "tu" (singular) / "voi" (plural). Just to be safe, you should address everyone else with the formal "Lei" (singular) / "Loro" (plural).

get a date

Looking to score? Try these.

| Hello, we haven't met. My name is ... | **Salve, non ci conosciamo. Sono ...**
sahlveh nohn chee kohnoh-shahmoh sohnoh
Direct and to the point. |

Are you alone?	**È solo ♂ / sola ♀ ?**
	eh sohloh / sohlah
	An obvious come-on—but virtually foolproof.

Would you like a drink?	**Vuole bere qualcosa?**
	voo-ohleh behreh kwahl-kohzah
	How can you say no?!

Wanna dance?	**Vuole ballare?**
	voo-ohleh bahl-lahreh
	Dancing is a popular pastime— you're certain to get a yes, "sì"!

| I'd love to have some company. | **Mi piacerebbe avere un po' di compagnia.** |
| | *me pee-ahche-rehb-beh ahvehreh oon poh dee kohmpah-nyah* |

Can we use "tu"?	**Posso darLe del tu?**
	pohs-soh dahrleh dehl too
	Go from being formal to informal with one simple question.

| You're special. | **Sei speciale.** |
| | *say spehchahleh* |

| You're sweet. | **Sei dolce.** |
| | *say dohl-cheh* |

| You're incredibly beautiful. | **Sei bellissimo ♂. / Sei bellissima ♀.** |
| | *say behl-lees-seemoh / say behl-lees-seemah* |

| You're not like other guys. | **Non sei come gli altri ♂.** |
| | *nohn say kohmeh lyee ahltree* |

yo! Too shy to approach that very attractive Italian? Try getting to know his or her friends and tell them what you think about that hottie.

That guy is …	**Quel tipo è …**
	kwehl *teep*oh eh
really amazing.	**troppo forte.**
	trohp-poh *fohr*teh
hot.	**un santo della Madonna.**
	oon *sahn*toh *dehl*-lah mah*dohn*-nah
	Literally: from the Madonna
really hot.	**uno schianto.**
	*oo*noh skee-*ahn*toh
That girl is …	**Quella tipa è …**
	kwehl-lah *teep*ah eh
incredibly beautiful.	**bellissima.**
	behl-*lees*-seemah
really hot.	**uno schianto.**
	*oo*noh skee-*ahn*toh
really sexy.	**una gran figa*.**
	*oo*nah grahn *fee*gah

*Guys may talk about a girl being a "figa", literally, *fig*, among themselves, but would never say it to a girl's face; it can be derogatory.

gay?

Looking for some alternative fun?

Are you gay?	**È gay?**
	eh gay

| Do you like *men / women*? | **Ti piacciono *gli uomini♂ / le donne♀*?** |
| | *tee pee-ah-tchohnoh lyee oo-ohmeenee / leh dohn-neh* |

| Let's go to a gay bar. | **Andiamo a un pub gay.** |
| | *ahndee-ahmoh ah oon pahb gay* |

He's <u>gay</u>.	**È …**
	eh
	omosessuale.
	ohmoh-sehs-soo-ahleh
	gay.
	gay
	diverso.
	deevehrsoh
	Literally: different

| She's a lesbian. | **È lesbica.** |
| | *eh lehzbeekah* |

She swings both ways.	**Le piace andare sia con gli uomini che con le donne.**
	leh pee-ahcheh ahndahreh see-ah kohn lyee oo-ohmeenee keh kohn leh dohn-neh
	Literally: She likes both men and women.

| He/She is bi. | **È bisex.** |
| | *eh beesex* |

Bologna is considered the "gay capital" of Italy. Many gay-friendly locations can also be found throughout Rome and its suburbs. Milan is another city in which gay bars and clubs thrive. For gay guys and lesbians who want to relax, try Versilia, an area in Tuscany that is gay-friendly; the same can be said about the coast of Romagna.

refusals

Not your type? Here are the best ways to reject someone.

I'm not in the right
mood tonight.

No, guarda, non è proprio serata.
*noh gwahrdah nohn eh prohpree-oh
sehrahtah*

Sorry, but I'm expecting
someone.

**Scusa, ma sto aspettando
qualcun altro.**
*skoozah mah stoh ahspeht-tahndoh
kwahlkoo-nahltroh*

Leave me alone!

Lasciami in pace!
lahshahmee een pahcheh

Get out of here!

Evapora!
ehvah-pohrah
Literally: Evaporate!

I'm busy.

Ho di meglio da fare.
oh dee mehlyoh dah fahreh
*Literally: I have something better
to do. Snobby, but it'll work.*

Take a hike!

Fa' / Fai dei metri!
fah / fah-ee day mehtree
*Drop the "i"-sound in "fai" to
sound really Italian!*

dating

Found an Italian lover? Here's how to describe your relationship.

We're having an affair.

Abbiamo una storia.
ahb-beeahmoh oonah stohree-ah

| We're going out. | **Ci vediamo. / Usciamo insieme.** |
| | *chee vehdee-ahmoh / ooshahmoh eensee-ehmeh* |

| He's my boyfriend. / She's my girlfriend. | **È il mio ragazzo♂. / È la mia ragazza♀.** |
| | *eh eel mee-oh rahgah-tzoh / eh lah mee-ah rah-gah-tzah* |

affection

Ask for some lovin'.

| Give me a kiss, baby. | **Dammi un bacio, tesoro.** |
| | *dahm-mee oon bah-choh tehzohroh* |

| I want you. | **Ho voglia di te.** |
| | *oh voh-lyah dee teh* |

| I want to make love to you. | **Voglio fare l'amore con te.** |
| | *voh-lyoh fahreh lahmohreh kohn teh* |

sex

A variety of ways to state the obvious…

| We had sex. | **Abbiamo fatto sesso.** |
| | *ahb-beeahmoh faht-toh sehs-soh* |

| We spent the night together. | **Abbiamo passato la notte assieme.** |
| | *ahb-beeahmoh pahs-sahtoh lah noht-teh ahs-see-ehmeh* |

We @#&!ed like rabbits.

Abbiamo trombato come ricci. 🌡️
ahb-bee<u>ah</u>moh trohm<u>bah</u>toh <u>koh</u>meh
<u>ree</u>-tchee
Literally: We @#&!ed like hedgehogs.

safe sex

Protection is a must, in any language.

Do you have a <u>condom</u>?

Hai un …?
<u>ahee</u> oon

preservativo
prehzehr-vah<u>tee</u>voh
The standard.

guanto
<u>gwahn</u>toh
Literally: glove
This is very casual—use it with someone you know very well!

goldone
gohl-<u>doh</u>neh
It's the slangy way to say it.

Are you on the pill?

Prendi la pillola?
<u>prehn</u>dee lah <u>peel</u>-lohlah

Did you put the diaphragm in?

Hai il diaframma?
<u>ahee</u> eel dee-ah<u>frahm</u>-mah

Do you use an IUD?

Hai la spirale?
<u>ahee</u> lah spee-<u>rah</u>leh

99

STDs

Don't get caught with your pants down.

He / She has a VD.

Quel tipo ♂/ Quella tipa ♀ ha una malattia venerea.
kwehl teepoh / kwehl-lah teepah ah oonah mahlaht-tee-ah vehneh-reh-ah

Have you had an AIDS test?

Hai fatto il test per l'aids?
ahee faht-toh eel tehst pehr lah-ee-dee-es-seh

Yeah, I'm clean.

Certo, tutto a posto.
chehrtoh toot-toh ah pohstoh

breaking up

Is that summer fling over? Say it!

I need some time to think.

Ho bisogno di tempo per riflettere.
oh beezohnyoh dee tehmpoh pehr reefleht-tehreh

Let's just be friends.

Rimaniamo amici.
reemahnee-ahmoh ahmeechee

It's better to break up.

È meglio farla finita.
eh mehlyoh fahrlah feeneetah

It's over between us.

È finita.
eh feeneetah

I'm over you!

Con te ho chiuso!
kohn teh oh kewzoh

100

where to shop

Grab your wallet and go!

Where's the main shopping area?	**Dov'è la zona dei negozi?** *doh<u>veh</u> lah <u>dzoh</u>nah day neh<u>goh</u>tzee*
Where's …?	**Dov'è …?** *doh<u>veh</u>*

the bookstore

> **la libreria**
> *lah leebreh<u>ree</u>-ah*

the department store

> **il grande magazzino**
> *eel <u>grahn</u>deh mahgah-<u>dzee</u>noh*

the drugstore

> **la farmacia**
> *lah fahrmah<u>chee</u>-ah*

the gift shop

> **il negozio di articoli da regalo**
> *eel neh<u>goh</u>tzee-oh dee ahr<u>tee</u>kohlee dah reh<u>gah</u>loh*

the health food store

> **il negozio di dietetica**
> *eel neh<u>goh</u>tzee-oh dee dee-eh<u>teh</u>-teeka*

the liquor store

> **l'enoteca**
> *lehnoh-<u>teh</u>kah*

the market

> **il mercato**
> *eel mehr<u>kah</u>toh*

the newsstand

> **l'edicola**
> *leh<u>dee</u>-kohlah*

the music store

> **il negozio di musica**
> *eel neh<u>goh</u>tzee-oh dee <u>moo</u>zeekah*

Where's …?	**Dov'è …?** *dohveh*
the souvenir store	**il negozio di souvenir** *eel nehgohtzee-oh dee soovehneer*
the sports store	**il negozio di articoli sportivi** *eel nehgohtzee-oh dee ahrteekohlee spohrteevee*
the supermarket	**il supermercato** *eel soopehr-mehrkahtoh*
When does the … *open / close*?	**Quando *apre / chiude* …?** *kwahndoh ahpreh / kewdeh*
Are you open in the evening?	**È aperto la sera?** *eh ah-pehrtoh lah sehrah*
Do you close for lunch?	**Chiude per pranzo?** *kewdeh pehr prahndzoh*

Visiting Italy in the summer? Plan ahead! During the month of August, most locals go to the sea or mountains to escape the humidity. In major cities like Rome, Milan, Bologna, and Florence, you might find few shops and restaurants open.

customer service

Need some assistance?

Where's the … department? **Dov'è il reparto …?**
dohveh eel rehpahrtoh

women's / men's **donna / uomo**
dohn-nah / oo-ohmoh

sportswear **articoli sportivi**
ahrteekohlee spohrteevee

shoe **calzature**
kahltzah-tooreh

cosmetics **cosmetici**
kohzmeh-teechee

Where's the fitting room? **Dove sono i camerini?**
dohveh sohnoh ee kahmeh-reenee

Where can I find …? **Dove sono …?**
dohveh sohnoh

books **i libri**
ee leebree

CDs **i CD**
ee chee dee

DVDs **i DVD**
ee dee voo dee

magazines **le riviste**
leh reeveesteh

postcards **le cartoline**
leh kahrtoh-leeneh

Looking for something in a particular color? Ask for it in…

beige	**beige** _behzh_	orange	**arancione** _ahrahn-chohneh_
black	**nero** _nehroh_	pink	**rosa** _rohzah_
blue	**blu** _bloo_	purple	**viola** _vee-ohlah_
brown	**marrone** _mahr-rohneh_	red	**rosso** _rohs-soh_
gray	**grigio** _greejoh_	white	**bianco** _bee-ahnkoh_
green	**verde** _vehrdeh_	yellow	**giallo** _jahl-loh_

sales help

Here's how to ask that cute salesperson for assistance.

Can you help me?

Può aiutarmi?
poo-oh ahyou-tahrmee

I'm looking for …

Cerco …
chehr-koh

Do you have …?

Avete …?
ahvehteh

I'd like to buy …

Vorrei comprare …
vohr-ray kohmprahreh

You may want to fill in those blanks with any of these items.

| baseball cap | **un cappellino con la visiera** |
| | *oon kahp-pehl-leenoh kohn lah veezee-ehrah* |

| bikini | **un bikini** |
| | *oon beekeenee* |

| bra | **un reggiseno** |
| | *oon rehdjee-sehnoh* |

| (push-up) bra | **un push-up** |
| | *oon poosh-ahp* |

| bracelet | **un braccialetto** |
| | *oon brah-tchahleht-toh* |

| briefs | **un paio di slip** |
| | *oon pahee-oh dee sleep* |

| earrings | **degli orecchini** |
| | *deh-lyee ohrehk-keenee* |

| flip-flops | **le ciabatte** |
| | *leh chahbaht-teh* |

| jacket | **una giacca** |
| | *oonah jahk-kah* |

| jeans | **un jeans** |
| | *oon jeans* |

| low-cut top | **un top scollato** |
| | *oon tohp skohl-lahtoh* |

| necklace | **una collana** |
| | *oonah kohl-lahnah* |

| panties | **una mutandina** |
| | *oonah moo-tahndeenah* |

| ring | **un anello** |
| | *oon ahnehl-loh* |

sandals	**i sandali**
	ee sahndahlee
skirt	**una gonna**
	oonah gohn-nah
sneakers	**le scarpe da tennis**
	leh skahrpeh dah tehn-nees
sweater	**una maglia**
	oonah mahlyah
swim shorts	**i calzoncini da bagno**
	ee kahltzohn-cheenee dah bahnyoh
swimsuit	**un costume da bagno**
	oon kohstoomeh dah bahnyoh
T-shirt	**una T-shirt / maglietta**
	oonah tee-shehrt / oonah mahlyeht-tah
watch	**un orologio da polso**
	oon ohroh-lohjoh dah pohlsoh

at the register

Looking to part with your hard-earned dough? Here's the lingo you need to make your purchase.

How much does it cost?

Quanto costa?
kwahntoh kohstah
You can also simply say, "Quant'è?"

Where do I pay?

Dove si paga?
dohveh see pahgah

I'll pay with a credit card.

Vorrei pagare con carta di credito.
vohr-ray pahgahreh kohn kahrtah dee krehdeetoh

107

| Do you accept travelers checks? | **Accetta traveler check?**
ah-tcheht-tah trah-vehl-lehr shehk |
| I'd like a receipt. | **Vorrei la ricevuta.**
vohr-ray lah reecheh-vootah
Just in case you need to return something... |

bargains

Put your negotiating skills to use.

That's too expensive.	**È troppo caro.** *eh trohp-poh kahroh*
Do you have anything cheaper?	**Ha qualcosa di più economico?** *ah kwahl-kohzah dee pew ehkoh-nohmeekoh*
I don't have enough cash.	**Non ho abbastanza contanti.** *nohn oh ahb-bahstahntzah kohntahntee*
I'll give you 10 euros.	**Facciamo 10 euro e non se ne parla più?** *fah-tchahmoh dee-ehchee eh-ooroh eh nohn seh neh pahrlah pew* *Literally: Should we make it 10€ and not speak of it any longer?*
This is a real bargain!	**È stato un affare!** *eh stahtoh oon ahf-fahreh*

the scoop

Feel free to bargain at flea markets, small mom n' pop stores, farmer's markets, and with street vendors who offer accessories and services just for tourists. Don't bargain in supermarkets and department stores—it won't work.

problems

Is there something wrong with your purchase?

This doesn't work.	**È difettoso ♂ / difettosa ♀.** *eh deefeht-<u>toh</u>zoh / deefeht-<u>toh</u>zah*
Can you exchange this, please?	**Può cambiarlo, per favore?** *poo-<u>oh</u> kahmbee-<u>ahr</u>loh pehr fah<u>voh</u>hreh*
I'd like a refund.	**Vorrei un rimborso.** *vohr-<u>ray</u> oon reem-<u>bohr</u>soh*
Here's the receipt.	**Ecco la ricevuta.** *<u>ehk</u>-koh lah reecheh-<u>voo</u>tah*
I don't have the receipt.	**Non ho la ricevuta.** *nohn oh lah reecheh-<u>voo</u>tah*

at the drugstore

Not feeling well? Here's some help.

Where's the nearest (all-night) pharmacy?	**Dov'è la farmacia (notturna) più vicina?** *doh<u>veh</u> lah fahrmah<u>chee</u>-ah (noht-<u>toor</u>-nah) pew vee<u>chee</u>nah*

What time does the pharmacy *open* / *close*?	**A che ora *apre* / *chiude* la farmacia?** *ah keh ohrah ahpreh / kewdeh lah fahrmahcheeah*
Can you fill this prescription for me?	**Può farmi questa ricetta?** *poo-oh fahr-me kwehstah reecheht-tah*
Should I wait?	**Devo aspettare?** *dehvoh ahspeht-tahreh*
I'll come back for it.	**Passerò a ritirarla.** *pahs-sehroh ah reetee-rahrlah*
How much should I take?	**Quanto devo prenderne?** *kwahntoh dehvoh prehn-dehrneh*
How often should I take it?	**Con quale frequenza devo prenderlo?** *kohn kwahleh freh-kwehntzah dehvoh prehn-dehrloh*
What would you recommend for …?	**Che cosa mi consiglia per …?** *keh kohzah me kohnsee-lyah pehr*
a cold	**un raffreddore** *oon rahf-frehd-dohreh*
a cough	**la tosse** *lah tohs-seh*
diarrhea	**la diarrea** *lah dee-ahr-reh-ah*
a hangover	**i postumi di una sbornia** *ee pohstoomee dee oonah zbohr-nee-ah*
hayfever	**la febbre da fieno** *lah fehb-breh dah fee-ehnoh*
insect bites	**le punture d'insetto** *leh poontooreh deenseht-toh*
a sore throat	**il mal di gola** *eel mahl dee gohlah*

| What would you recommend for …? | **Che cosa mi consiglia per …?** |
| | *keh kohzah me kohnsee-lyah pehr* |

| sunburn | **l'eritema solare** |
| | *lehree-tehmah sohlahreh* |

| motion sickness | **la cinetosi** |
| | *lah cheeneh-tohzee* |

| an upset stomach | **il mal di stomaco** |
| | *eel mahl dee stohmahkoh* |

| Can I have …? | **Ha …?** |
| | *ah* |

| antiseptic cream | **una pomata antisettica** |
| | *oonah pohmahtah ahntee-seht-teekah* |

| aspirin | **dell'aspirina** |
| | *dehl-lah-speereenah* |

| bandages | **delle bende** |
| | *dehl-leh behndeh* |

| condoms | **dei profilattici** |
| | *day prohfeelaht-teechee* |

| insect repellent | **un repellente per insetti** |
| | *oon rehpehl-lehnteh pehr eenseht-tee* |

| painkillers | **un analgesico** |
| | *oon ahnahl-jehzeekoh* |

| vitamins | **delle vitamine** |
| | *dehl-leh veetah-meeneh* |

FACT Pharmacies are easily recognized by their sign: a green cross, usually lit up. If you are looking for a pharmacy at night, on Sundays, or holidays, you'll find the address of emergency pharmacies, "farmacia di turno", listed in the newspaper or displayed in pharmacy windows.

toiletries

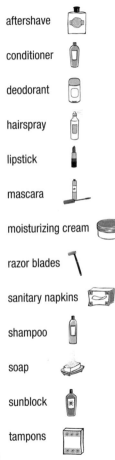

aftershave	**un dopobarba** *oon dohpoh-bahrbah*
conditioner	**del balsamo** *dehl bahlsahmoh*
deodorant	**un deodorante** *oon deh-ohdoh-rahnteh*
hairspray	**della lacca per capelli** *dehl-lah lahk-kah pehr kahpehl-lee*
lipstick	**un rossetto** *oon rohs-seht-toh*
mascara	**un mascara** *oon mahskahrah*
moisturizing cream	**una crema idratante** *oonah krehmah eedrah-tahnteh*
razor blades	**delle lamette da barba** *dehl-leh lahmeht-teh dah bahrbah*
sanitary napkins	**degli assorbenti** *deh-lyee ahs-sohrbehntee*
shampoo	**dello shampoo** *dehl-loh shahm-poh*
soap	**del sapone** *dehl sahpohneh*
sunblock	**un solare** *oon sohlahreh*
tampons	**dei tamponi** *day tahmpohnee*

tissues		**dei fazzoletti di carta** *day fah-tzohleht-tee dee kahrtah*
toilet paper		**della carta igienica** *dehl-lah kahrtah eejeh-neekah*
toothpaste		**un dentifricio** *oon dehntee-freechoh*

the scoop

For the ultimate in fine Italian perfumes, lotions, powders, and other toiletries, don't miss the "Farmacia Santa Maria Novella" in Florence. Originally founded by Dominican friars, this pharmacy has been making handcrafted products for Italian nobility and royalty since the 1600s. Even if you're not into the beauty products, you'll be wowed by the setting— an 18th-century building decorated with frescoes, antique furniture, and authentic gizmos from the original workshop.

camera shop

Admit it, you're a tourist. You'll need these.

Where's the camera shop? **Dov'è il negozio di foto?**
dohveh eel nehgohtzee-oh dee fohtoh

I'm looking for a
disposable camera.
**Cerco una macchina fotografica
usa-e-getta.**
chehr-koh oonah mahk-keenah fohtoh-grahfeekah oozah eh jeht-tah

113

Do you sell ... for digital cameras?	**Avete ... per fotocamere digitali?** *ah<u>veh</u>teh ... pehr fohtoh-<u>kah</u>mehreh deejee-<u>tah</u>lee*
memory cards	**schede di memoria** *<u>skeh</u>deh dee meh-<u>moh</u>ree-ah*
batteries	**batterie** *baht-teh<u>ree</u>-eh*
I'd like this film developed.	**Vorrei far sviluppare questa pellicola.** *<u>vohr</u>-ray fahr sveeloop-<u>pah</u>reh <u>kweh</u>stah pehl-<u>lee</u>kohlah* *You're old school, aren't you?!*
When will the photos be ready?	**Quando saranno pronte le foto?** *<u>kwahn</u>doh sah<u>rahn</u>-noh <u>prohn</u>teh leh <u>foh</u>toh*
I'd like to pick up my photos.	**Vorrei ritirare le mie foto.** *<u>vohr</u>-ray reetee-<u>rah</u>reh leh <u>me</u>-eh <u>foh</u>toh*

internet café

Stay in touch with friends and family at home.

Where is there an internet café near here? | **Dov'è un Internet cafè qui vicino?**
dohveh oon eentehrneht kahfeh kwee veecheenoh

Can I access the internet here? | **Posso connettermi qui?**
pohs-soh kohn-neht-tehrmee kwee

How much is it for an hour? | **Quanto costa all'ora?**
kwahntoh kohstah ahl-lohrah

Turn on the computer. | **Accendi il computer.**
ah-tchehn-dee eel kohm-pewtehr

Can I connect [to the internet] on this computer? | **Posso connettermi con questo computer?**
pohs-soh kohn-neht-tehrmee kohn kwehstoh kohm-pewtehr

Can I check my e-mail? | **Posso controllare le mie mail?**
pohs-soh kohntrohl-lahreh leh me-eh mehl

Can I download some stuff? | **Posso scaricare della roba?**
pohs-soh skahree-kahreh dehl-lah rohbah

I'm *surfing the web / online.* | **Sono in *rete / online.***
sohnoh een rehteh / ohnlah-een

 Where is that internet café? For up-to-the-minute info on locations, try an online search. If you're already in Italy, find the local Tourist Information Office; it'll provide you with names, addresses, and directions for cybercafés. Worst comes to worst, walk around and read the signs. You're bound to find a few in every city and town.

computer crash

Instant IT help…

This computer froze.

Il computer si è bloccato.
eel kohm-pewtehr see eh blohk-kahtoh

This computer is dead.

Il computer non dà segni di vita.
eel kohm-pewtehr nohn dah sehnyee dee veetah
Literally: This computer doesn't show any signs of life.

The file is lost.

Il file è andato perso.
eel fah-eel eh ahndahtoh pehrsoh

laptop

Brought your own laptop? You might need these questions.

Does this *hotel / café* have Wi-Fi®?

Questo *albergo / café* ha l'accesso Wi-Fi® a Internet?
kwehstoh ahlbehrgoh / kahfeh ah lah-tchehs-soh oo-ah-ee fah-ee ah eentehrneht

Where is the closest hotspot?

Dov'è la connessione Wi-Fi® più vicina?
dohveh lah kohn-nehs-seeohneh oo-ah-ee fah-ee pew veecheenah

Is there a connection fee?

Bisogna pagare per la connessione?
beezohnyah pahgahreh pehr lah kohn-nehs-seeohneh

Do I have to register?

Bisogna registrarsi?
beezohnyah rehjee-strahrsee

go!

Sitting next to a cutie at an Italian internet café or Wi-Fi® area? Spark his or her interest with these.

Are you online?	**Stai navigando?** *stah-ee nahvee-gahndoh*
That's my favorite site.	**È il mio sito preferito.** *eh eel mee-oh seetoh prefeh-reetoh*
Can you send me that link?	**Puoi mandarmi il link?** *poo-oh-ee mahndahrme eel leenk*
I love to chat!	**Mi piace un sacco chattare!** *me pee-ahcheh oon sahk-koh chaht-tahreh*
Can you give me your e-mail?	**Mi dai la tua mail?** *me dah-ee lah too-ah mehl*

instant messaging

Do you require instant gratification?

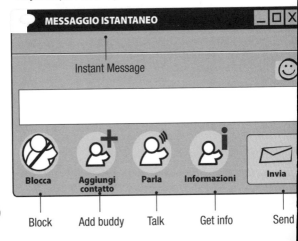

MESSAGGIO ISTANTANEO

Instant Message

Blocca	Aggiungi contatto	Parla	Informazioni	Invia
Block	Add buddy	Talk	Get info	Send

chat room

When visiting a chat room, "una chat", "una stanza chat", or "una chat-room", keep in mind these abbreviations and expressions.

Female or male?	**F O M?**
next	**PROX**
kiss	**SMACK**
I love you.	**TVB [Ti voglio bene.]**
Let's speak privately.	**PVT [parlare in privato]**
Where RU?	**DGT [Da dove digiti?]** *Literally: Where are you connecting from?*
to, for	**X [per]**
more	**+ [più]**
anyway	**CMQ [comunque]**

phone call

From public to private, the language you need to make your call.

Can I have your phone number?	**Mi dà il Suo numero di telefono?** *me dah eel soo-oh noomehroh dee tehleh-fohnoh*
Here's my number.	**Ecco il mio numero.** *ehk-koh eel me-oh noomehroh*
Please call me.	**Mi chiami, La prego.** *me kee-ahmee lah prehgoh*

I'll give you a call.	**La chiamerò.** *lah kee-ahmeh<u>roh</u>*
Where's the nearest phone booth?	**Dov'è il telefono pubblico più vicino?** *doh<u>veh</u> eel teh<u>leh</u>-fohnoh <u>poob</u>-bleekoh pew vee<u>chee</u>noh*
May I use your phone?	**Posso usare il Suo telefono?** *<u>pohs</u>-soh oo<u>zah</u>reh eel <u>soo</u>-oh teh<u>leh</u>-fohnoh*
It's an emergency.	**È una emergenza.** *eh oonehmehr-<u>jehn</u>tzah*
What's the area code for …?	**Qual è il prefisso per …?** *kwah<u>leh</u> eel preh<u>fees</u>-soh pehr*
I'd like a phone card.	**Vorrei una carta telefonica.** *<u>vohr</u>-ray <u>oo</u>nah <u>kahr</u>tah tehleh<u>foh</u>-neekah*
What's the number for Information?	**Qual è il numero del Servizio Informazioni?** *kwah<u>leh</u> eel <u>noo</u>mehroh dehl sehr<u>veet</u>zee-oh eenfohr-mahtzee-<u>ohnee</u>*
I'd like to call collect.	**Vorrei fare una telefonata a carico del destinatario.** *<u>vohr</u>-ray <u>fah</u>reh <u>oo</u>nah tehleh-foh<u>nah</u>tah ah <u>kah</u>reekoh dehl deh-steenah-<u>tah</u>ree-oh*
Hi. This is …	**Salve, sono …** *<u>sahl</u>veh <u>soh</u>noh*
Hello?	**Pronto?** *<u>prohn</u>toh* *Literally: Ready?*
Yes?	**Sì?** *see*

120

Who's speaking?	**Chi parla?** *key pahrlah*
It's me.	**Sono io.** *sohnoh ee-oh*
Could I speak to … please?	**Mi passa … per favore?** *mee pahs-sah … pehr fahvohreh*
Just a minute.	**Un attimo solo.** *oon aht-teemoh sohloh*
Speak louder, please.	**Parli più forte, per piacere.** *pahrlee pew fohrteh pehr pee-ahchehreh*
Speak more slowly, please.	**Parli più lentamente, per piacere.** *pahrlee pew lehntah-mehnteh pehr pee-ahchehreh*
Would you ask him / her to call me?	**Può dirgli ♂ / dirle ♀ di richiamarmi?** *poo-oh deer-lyee / deer-leh dee ree-kee-ahmahrmee*
Call me!	**Chiamami!** *kee-ahmahmee* *If you're talking to anyone other than friends or family, use the formal: "Mi chiami!"*

hangin' up

Say good-bye with grace.

Sorry, gotta go.	**Scusa, ma devo andare.** *skoozah mah dehvoh ahndahreh* *Say "scusi" if the situation requires politeness.*

I have to be off!	**Devo scappare!** *dehvoh skahp-pahreh*
Call me later!	**Fammi uno squillo più tardi!** *fahm-me oonoh skweel-loh pew tahrdee* *Use this with relatives and close friends.*
Will you send me a kiss before you hang up?	**Me lo mandi un bacio prima di riattaccare?** *meh loh mahndee oon bah-choh preemah dee ree-aht-tahk-kahreh*

text messaging

Send someone you love an SMS.

Where are you?	**Dove 6? [Dove sei?]** *"Sei", the number six, is spelled the same as "sei", you are.*
Let's talk later!	**C sent + tardi! [Ci sentiamo più tardi!]**
CUL8TR [See you later.]	**C ved dopo! [Ci vediamo dopo!]**
Why didn't you come?	**Xké nn 6 venuto? [Perché non sei venuto?]**
I love you so much.	**TAT [Ti amo tanto.]**

Text Message	Italian Equivalent	English Translation
Dove 6?	**Dove sei?**	Where RU? (Where are you?)
Ho da fare. C sent + tardi!	**Ho da fare. Ci sentiamo più tardi!**	I'm busy. Let's talk later!

the scoop

It seems that just about everyone in Italy—adults, teens, and kids—has a wireless phone. Some even have two! Though making and receiving calls remains fairly expensive, it's one of the most popular forms of communication. Wireless phones are so popular that it's important to personalize them with unique colors, designs, and even ring tones, "suonerie".

Haven't used a public phone in a while, huh?! You can find public telephones just about anywhere in most Italian cities. Coin-operated phones are pretty rare, though, so you'll need to buy a "carta telefonica", phone card, to use the public phones. You can buy one at "tabacchi", tobacco shops, and be able to talk for up to three hours for as little as 5 euros—just make sure you buy one specifically for the country you're calling. Before you can use the card, you have to tear off the corner, marked with a dotted line, or the card won't work. As you talk, keep an eye on the computerized monitor to watch your minutes (or euros) ticking away—you wouldn't want to get cut off! Warning: Do not make calls using the 800 numbers posted on the public phone booths. Even though they may look official, and are sometimes actually installed under plastic coverings, their rates can be very high. Also avoid making calls from your hotel room. A surcharge is almost always added, and it can be hefty!

To make an international call, dial 00 + country code + area code + number. Country codes: Australia, 61; UK, 44; US and Canada, 1

snail mail

Wanna mail your stuff the old-fashioned way?

Where is the nearest post office?	**Dov'è l'ufficio postale più vicino?** *doh<u>veh</u> loof-<u>fee</u>choh poh<u>stah</u>leh pew vee<u>chee</u>noh*
What time does the post office *open / close*?	**A che ora *apre / chiude* l'ufficio postale?** *ah keh <u>oh</u>rah* <u>ah</u>preh / <u>kew</u>deh *loof-<u>fee</u>choh poh<u>stah</u>leh*
Does it close for lunch?	**Chiude per pranzo?** *<u>kew</u>deh pehr <u>prahn</u>dzoh*
Where's the mailbox?	**Dov'è la cassetta delle lettere?** *doh<u>veh</u> lah kahs-<u>sah</u>tah <u>dehl</u>-leh <u>leht</u>-tehreh*
A stamp for this postcard, please.	**Un francobollo per questa cartolina, per favore.** *oon frahnkoh-<u>bohl</u>-loh pehr <u>kweh</u>stah kahrtoh-<u>lee</u>neh pehr fah<u>voh</u>reh*

the scoop

Think snail-mail is too last-century? Italy's post office offers a variety of online services for the tech-savvy postal customer. You can send personalized online postcards for free. If you're writing to someone within Italy, you can also type your letter online and the post office will print and deliver your letter. Keep in mind, though, the website, **http://www.poste.it/online/postali**, is only in Italian.

DICTIONARY
Italian ▸ English

A

abbastanza enough

abboccato *m* semi-dry (wine)

abbuffata *f* feast (large meal)

accendere to turn on, to light up

accesso wireless a Internet *m* Wi-Fi® area

acqua *f* water

affare *m* bargain

affumicato *m* / **affumicata** *f* smoked

aggiungere to add

aggressione per rapina *f* mugging

agnello *m* lamb

aiutare to help

aiuto *m* help

albergo *m* hotel

allora so, then, well, therefore

altro *m* / **altra** *f* other, another, more, further, different

amabile *m* slightly sweet (wine)

amaro *m* / **amara** *f* bitter

amico *m* / **amica** *f* friend

ammobiliato *m* / **ammobiliata** *f* furnished

amore *m* love

analgesico *m* painkiller

ananas *m* pineapple

anatra *f* duck

ancora again, still, yet, more

andare to go

andata *f* one way

andata *f* **e ritorno** *m* round trip

anello *m* ring

anguilla *f* eel

anguria *f* watermelon

annegare to drown

anticipo *m* deposit

antipasto *m* hors d'oeuvre

aperitivo *m* before-dinner alcoholic drink

aperto *m* / **aperta** *f* open

aprire to open

arancia *f* orange

aria *f* air

aria condizionata *f* air conditioning

arrivare to arrive

arrivi (on sign) arrivals

Arrivederci! Good-bye!

arrosto *m* / **arrosta** *f* roasted

asciugamano *m* towel

aspettare to wait

assicurazione *f* insurance

assieme together

assorbente *m* sanitary napkin

attimo *m* moment

attrezzature *f pl* facilities

attrezzature da sub *f pl* diving equipment

avere to have

avere bisogno di to need

avere un guasto to break down (car)

B

baciare to kiss

bacio *m* kiss

bagagli *m pl* luggage

bagnino *m* life guard

bagno *m* bath, bathroom

bagno turco *m* steam room

ballare to dance

balsamo *m* conditioner (hair care)

bancomat *m* ATM

barca a motore *f* motorboat

barca *f* boat

batteria *f* battery

bellissimo *m* / **bellissima** *f* very beautiful

bello *m* / **bella** *f* beautiful, hottie

bende *f pl* bandages

bene well, good

benzina *f* gasoline

bere to drink

bevanda *f* drink

biancheria da letto *f* bedding

bianco *m* / **bianca** *f* white

bibita *f* drink (alcoholic or non-alcoholic)

biblioteca *f* library

bicchiere *m* glass

bici *f* bike

biglietteria *f* ticket office, box office

biglietto *m* ticket

biglietto d'ingresso *m* entrance fee

binario *m* platform

birra *f* beer

birra alla spina *f* draft beer

biscotto *m* cookie

bistecca *f* steak

bloccato frozen (computer)

blu *m* / *f* blue (dark)

bottiglia *f* bottle

bracciale *m* bracelet

brutto *m* / **brutta** *f* ugly, unattractive

Buona notte! Good night!

Buonasera! Good evening!

Buongiorno! Good morning!

buonissimo *m* / **buonissima** *f* very good

buono *m* / **buona** *f* good

burro *m* butter

C

calcio *m* soccer, kick

caldo *m* / **calda** *f* warm, hot

calzature *f pl* shoes

calzoncini da bagno *m pl* swimming trunks

cambiare to change

cambio *m* change, exchange

camera *f* room

camerino *m* fitting room

campeggio *m* camping

capelli *m pl* hair

capezzolo *m* nipple

capire to understand

cappuccio *m* (slang) condom

caraffa *f* carafe

carciofo *m* artichoke

caricare to upload, overload

carino *m* / **carina** *f* cute, charming, pretty

caro *m* / **cara** *f* dear, expensive

carro attrezzi tow truck

carta *f* paper

carta igienica *f* toilet paper

cartolina *f* postcard

casino *m* a lot

cassa *f* cashier, counter

cassaforte *f* safe (for valuables)

cassetta delle lettere *f* mailbox

castello *m* castle

cavolo *m* cabbage

cena *f* dinner, supper

centro città *m* town center

cercare to look for

cerchio *m* circle

Certo! Sure!

che that, which, what

chi who, whom

chiamata *f* call

chiappe *f pl* (slang) butt (bottom)

chiave *f* key

chiesa *f* church

chilometraggio *m* mileage

chiudere to close

chiuso *m* / chiusa *f* closed

ciabatte *f pl* slippers, flip flops

cibo *m* food

cifra *f* amount (money)

ciliege *f pl* cherries

cimitero *m* cemetery

cinetosi *f* motion sickness (air, water, car)

cinque five

cioccolata calda *f* hot chocolate

cipolla *f* onion

città *f* town, city

città vecchia *f* old town

cocomero *m* watermelon

Coglione! (slang) You dick!

colazione *f* breakfast

collana *f* necklace

coltello *m* knife

come like, as

Come? How?

cominciare to begin

commissariato *m* police station

compagnia *f* company

comprare to buy

compreso *m* / compresa *f* included

con with

confermare to confirm

coniglio *m* rabbit

connessione wireless *f* hotspot (Wi-Fi® area)

conoscere to know (a place, a person)

consigliare to recommend

cosa *f* thing

contanti *m pl* cash

contenere to contain

conto *m* account, bill, check

controllare to check

coperta *f* blanket

coperto *m* (ristorante) cover charge

corposo *m* full-bodied (wine)

Cosa? What?

così thus, this way

costume da bagno *m* swimsuit

cotoletta *f* cutlet

crema idratante *f* moisturizing cream

cucchiaio *m* spoon

cucinare to cook

cuffie *f pl* headphones

culo *m* ass

cuscino *m* pillow, cushion

cyclette *f* stationary bike

D

danneggiare to damage

dare to give

dentifricio *m* toothpaste

dentro inside

denunciare to report

deposito bagagli automatico *m* lockers

deposito bagagli *m* baggage room

diaframma *m* diaphragm

diarrea *f* diarrhea

dieci ten

difettoso *m* / **difettosa** *f* defective

digestivo *m* after-dinner alcoholic drink

discoteca *f* club

diverso *m* / **diversa** *f* different

divino *m* / **divina** *f* heavenly, divine

DOC guaranteed origin (wine)

doccia *f* shower

dolce *m* dessert

dolce *m* / *f* sweet

domani tomorrow

donna *f* woman

dopo after, later

dopobarba *m* aftershave

doppiato *m* dubbed

doppio *m* / **doppia** *f* double

Dov'è? Where is?

due two

duro *m* / **dura** *f* hard

E

economia *f* **e commercio** *m* business (area of studies)

edicola *f* newsagent

emergenza *f* emergency

enoteca *f* liquor store

eritema solare *m* sunburn

errore *m* mistake

essere to be

extracomunitario *m* / **extracomunitaria** *f* non-EU citizen

F

fagioli *m pl* beans

fare to do, to make

fare l'amore to make love

fare una passeggiata to go for a walk

fare uno squillo to call (phone)

farla finita to break up

farmacia *m* pharmacy, drugstore
fastidio *m* nuisance
fazzoletto *m* handkerchief, tissue
febbre da fieno *f* hay fever
fermare to stop
fermata *f* stop
festa *f* holiday, party
figlio *m* / **figlia** *f* son / daughter
figlio *m* / **figlia** *f* **di puttana** (slang)
  son of a bitch
figo *m* (slang) cool
finestra *f* window
finestrino *m* window (car, train,
  airplane, etc.)
finire to finish, to run out
fisso *m* / **fissa** *f* set, firm
forchetta *f* fork
formaggio *m* cheese
forte *m* / *f* strong, loud, cool
Forza! Go for it!
fra between, among
fragola *f* strawberry
francobollo *m* stamp
fratello *m* brother
freddo *m* / **fredda** *f* cold
fresco *m* / **fresca** *f* fresh
fritto *m* / **fritta** *f* fried
frizzante *m* / *f* sparkling
frutta *f* fruit
fumare to smoke
fumatore *m* / **fumatrice** *f* smoker
fungo *m* mushroom
funzionare to work (function)
fuoco *m* fire

fuori outside
furto *m* theft

G

gabinetto *m* restroom / toilet
gambero *m* shrimp
gelateria *f* ice-cream parlor
genitori *m pl* parents
già already
giacca *f* jacket
giallo *m* / **gialla** *f* yellow
giardino *m* garden
giorno *m* day
goccio *m* shot (drink)
gonna *f* skirt
granchio *m* crab
grande *m* / *f* big, large
grande magazzino *m* department
  store
grasso *m* / **grassa** *f* fat
grazie thank you
grigio *m* / **grigia** *f* gray / grey
grosso *m* / **grossa** *f* large
guanto *m* glove
guardare to watch, to look

I

ieri yesterday
in orario on time
incassare to cash
incidente *m* accident
incontrarsi to meet with someone
indirizzo *m* address (postal and
  e-mail)
Inghilterra *f* England

inglese *m / f* English
ingresso *m* entry, entrance
insieme together
interesse *m* interest
investire to run someone over, to run into someone
inviare to send
IVA *f* Value Added Tax

L

là over there
labbra *f pl* lips
lacca *f* hair spray
ladro *m* thief
lago *m* lake
lametta da barba *f* razor blade
lamponi *m pl* raspberries
lasciare to leave
lasciare libera la camera to check out (hotel)
latte *m* milk
lattuga *f* lettuce
lavorare to work
lavoro *m* work
leggere to read
leggero *m / * **leggera** *f* light (weight)
lei she
lentamente slowly
lento *m / * **lenta** *f* slow
lesbica *f* lesbian
letto *m* bed
lettore di MP3 *m* MP3 player
libero *m / * **libera** *f* free

libreria *f* bookstore
libro *m* book
limonata *f* lemonade
locale *m* spot (club, pub, etc.)
lontano *m / * **lontana** *f* far
loro they
luce *f* light
lui he
lumache *f pl* snails
luna *f* moon

M

macchina *f* car
macchina fotografica *f* camera
madre *f* mother
magazzino *m* warehouse
maglia *f* sweater
maglietta *f* T-shirt
maiale *m* pig, pork
mal di gola *m* sore throat
mal di stomaco *m* stomachache
malattia *f* disease
male badly, poorly
mancia *f* tip
mandare to send
mangiare to eat
manifestazione event
mano *f* hand
manzo *m* beef
mappa *f* map
marmellata *f* jam, marmalade
marrone *m / f* brown
mattina *f* morning
meglio better

mento *m* chin

meraviglioso *m* / **meravigliosa** *f* amazing

mercato *m* market

merda *f* shit

merda, di *m* / *f* shitty

merluzzo *m* cod

mettere to put

miele *m* honey

minestra *f* soup

morire to die

moto d'acqua *f* jet-ski

moto *f* motorcycle

motorino *m* moped

mutandina *f* panties

N

naso *m* nose

naturale (acqua) *f* still (water)

negozio *m* shop

negozio di articoli da regalo *m* gift shop

negozio di articoli sportivi *m* sports store

negozio di dietetica *m* health food store

negozio di foto *m* camera shop

negozio di musica *m* music store

negozio di souvenir *m* souvenir store

nero *m* / **nera** *f* black

noi we

noioso *m* / **noiosa** *f* boring

noleggiare to rent, to hire

notte *f* night

nove nine

numero *m* number

nuotare to swim

O

oasi naturale *f* nature preserve

occupato *m* / **occupata** *f* occupied, taken

oggi *m* today

ombelico *m* belly button

ombrellone *m* beach umbrella

omosessuale *m* / *f* gay

ora *f* hour, time

ora now

orario *m* timetable, schedule

orario di apertura *m* operating hours

ordinare to order

orecchino *m* earring

orecchio *m* ear

orologio *m* clock

orologio da polso *m* wristwatch

orrendo *m* / **orrenda** *f* horrible

ospite *m* / *f* guest

osteria *f* tavern

otto eight

P

padre *m* father

paese *m* country, small town

pagare to pay

paglia *f* (slang) cigarette

palazzo *m* palace

palestra *f* gym

pancetta *f* bacon

pane *m* bread

pane tostato *m* toast

panino *m* bread roll, sandwich

paninoteca *f* sandwich bar

parco *m* park

parlare to speak, to talk

partenze (on sign) departures

partire to leave, to depart

partita *f* game (sports), match

passaggio *m* ride

passare to pass, spend (time)

peperone *m* pepper (vegetable)

per for, to

per piacere please

pera *f* pear

perché why, because

Permesso? May I?

perso *m* / **persa** *f* lost

pesca *f* peach

pesce *m* fish

pesce spada swordfish

pezzo *m* piece

piacere to like

piano slowly, softly

piatti tipici *m pl* typical dishes

piatto *m* dish, plate

pieno *m* full tank

pieno *m* / **piena** *f* full

pillola *f* pill

piscina *f* swimming pool

piselli *m pl* peas

poco a little

polipo *m* octopus

pollo *m* chicken

pomata antisettica *f* antiseptic ointment

pomodoro *m* tomato

pompelmo *m* grapefruit

portare to bring, to take, to carry

posto *m* space, place, seat

postumi di una sbornia *f* hangover

pranzo *m* lunch

precedenza *f* right of way

preferito *m* / **preferita** *f* favorite

prefisso *m* area code

Prego! / Prego? You're welcome! / I beg your pardon?

prelievo *m* withdrawal (bank)

prendere to take, to seize

prenotazione *f* reservation

presto quickly, early

presto, a see you soon

prezzo *m* price

prima before, earlier

primo *m* / **prima** *f* first

profilattico *m* condom

pronto *m* / **pronta** *f* ready

Pronto? Hello? (telephone)

prosciutto cotto / crudo cooked ham / air cured ham

prossimo *m* / **prossima** *f* next

pulito *m* / **pulita** *f* clean

puntare su to bet on

puntata *f* bet

punture d'insetto *f pl* insect bites

Q

qua here
quadrato *m* square
qualche *m* / *f* some
qualcosa *m* / *f* something, anything
qualcuno *m* / *f* someone
quale *m* / *f* which
quando when
Quant'è? How much is it?
quanto how much / many, how long
quattro four
quello *m* / **quella** *f* that
questo *m* / **questa** *f* this
qui here

R

raffreddore *m* cold (sickness)
ragazza *f* girl, girlfriend
ragazzo *m* boy, boyfriend
regalo *m* gift
reggiseno *m* bra
registrarsi to register
reparto *m* department
repellente per insetti *m* insect repellent
resto *m* change (money)
riattaccare to hang up (telephone)
ricetta *f* prescription, recipe
ricevuta *f* receipt
ridere to laugh
riduzione *f* discount
riflettere to think

rimborso *m* refund
rimettere to throw up
ripetere to repeat
riscaldamento *m* heating
riso *m* rice
ritardo *m* delay
ritirare to pick up
rivista *f* magazine
roba *f* stuff
robusto *m* / **robusta** *f* sturdy, hefty
rompere to break
rosa *m* / *f* pink
rosato *m* rosé (wine)
rossetto *f* lipstick
rosso *m* / **rossa** *f* red
rotolo *m* roll, coil
rotto *m* / **rotta** *f* broken
rubare to steal
rubato *m* / **rubata** *f* stolen
rubinetto *m* faucet / tap
rumore *m* noise
rumoroso *m* / **rumorosa** *f* noisy

S

sabbia *f* sand
sacchetto *m* bag (plastic, paper)
sagra *f* festival
sala *f* hall
saldo *m* sale (discount)
sale *m* salt
salire to climb, to get on / in, to go up
salita *f* slope, ascent
salotto *m* sitting room
saltare to jump

133

salutare to greet

Salute! Cheers! / Bless you! (sneezing)

Salve! Hello!

sandali *m pl* sandals

sapere to know

sapone *m* soap

sapore *m* flavor

sasso *m* stone, rock

sbagliato *m* / **sbagliata** *f* wrong

sbornia *f* hangover

scalata *f* climbing

scale *f pl* stairs

scappare to flee, to rush

scaricare to download

scarpa *f* shoe

scarpe da tennis *f pl* sneakers

scatola *f* box

scemo *m* / **scema** *f* fool

scendere to get off

scheda di memoria *f* memory card

scheda (telefonica) *f* phone card

schermo *m* screen

schianto *m* a knockout

schifo *m* disgust

sci *m* ski

sci d'acqua *m pl* waterskis

sci nautico *m* waterskiing

sciare to ski

sciarpa *f* scarf

scienze *f pl* sciences

sciocco *m* / **sciocca** *f* foolish

sciogliere to dissolve, to melt

sciopero *m* strike (work)

sciroppo *m* syrup

scollato *m* / **scollata** *f* low-cut

scomodo *m* / **scomoda** *f* uncomfortable

sconto *m* discount

scontrino *m* purchase receipt

Scozia *f* Scotland

scrivere to write

scuro *m* / **scura** *f* dark

Scusi! / Scusa! Excuse me! *also* I'm sorry!

secco *m* / **secca** *f* dry

sedersi to sit

sedia a sdraio deck chair

sedia *f* chair

segnale *m* sign

sei six

seno *m* breast

sentire to hear, to feel

senza without

sera *f* evening

serata *f* evening

serio *m* / **seria** *f* serious

serratura *f* lock

servizio *m* service

sesso *m* sex

seta *f* silk

sete *f* thirst

sette seven

settimana *f* week

sfiga *f* (slang) rotten luck

sicurezza *f* safety, security, certainty

sicuro *m* / **sicura** *f* safe, sure

siga *f* cigarette

sigaretta *f* cigarette

significare to mean

simpatico *m* / **simpatica** *f* likeable, agreeable, cute

singolo *m* / **singola** *f* single

sito *m* site

slip *m* briefs

smettere to stop

snello *m* / **snella** *f* slim

soffocare to suffocate

sogliola *f* sole (fish)

sognare to dream

solare *m* sunblock

soldi *m pl* money

solo *m* / **sola** *f* alone

sopra on; over

sopracciglia *f pl* eyebrows

soprattutto especially

sorella *f* sister

sorriso *m* smile

sostare to stand, to stop (a car)

sotto under

sottotitoli *m pl* subtitles

spazzola *f* brush (hair, clothes)

spazzolino *m* toothbrush

specialista *m* / *f* specialist

spegnere to switch off, to put out

spesso often

spiacente *m* / *f* sorry

spiaggia *f* beach

spiccioli *m pl* change (small coins)

spingere to push

spogliatoio *m* changing room

sporco *m* / **sporca** *f* dirty

sportello *m* door, counter, window (office)

sposato *m* / **sposata** *f* married

spugna *f* sponge

spuntino *m* snack

squisito *m* / **squisita** *f* delicious, exquisite

stampare to print

stanza *f* room

stare male to feel sick

stasera tonight

stazione di servizio *f* gas station

sterlina *f* pound (British currency)

stivale *m* boot

storia *f* affair

strada *f* street, road

straniero *m* / **straniera** *f* foreign, foreigner

strano *m* / **strana** *f* strange

studiare to study

stupro *m* rape

su on, up

succo *m* juice

suonare to play (an instrument)

supermercato *m* supermarket

sveglia *f* alarm clock, wake-up call

svegliare to wake (someone) up

svendita *f* liquidation sale, clearance

sviluppare to develop

135

T

taglia *f* size (clothing)
tagliare to cut
talvolta sometimes
tamponi *m pl* tampons
tanto much, a lot
tappeto *m* rug; mat
tardi late
tariffe speciali *f pl* discounts
tasca *f* pocket
tatuaggio *m* tattoo
tavola da surf *f* surfboard
tavolo *m* table
tazza *f* cup
tè *m* tea
telefonata *f* telephone call
telefonata a carico del destinatario *f* collect call
telefono pubblico *m* phone booth
tempo *m* time
tenda *f* tent, curtain
tenere to keep, to hold
terra *f* earth, soil, ground
tesoro *m / f* baby, honey
testa *f* head
tette *f pl* (slang) boobs
tirare to pull
tiro *m* drag (smoke)
toast *m* hot sandwich with ham and cheese
toccare to touch
tonno *m* tuna
torcia *f* flashlight

tosse *f* cough
tovagliolo *m* napkin
tra between, among
tradurre to translate
traghetto *m* ferry
tranquillo *m / ***tranquilla** *f* quiet
trattamento del viso *m* facial
tre three
treno *m* train
triste *m / f* sad
troppo too, too much
trota *f* trout
trovare to find
trucco *m* make-up
tu you (sing.)
tuffarsi to dive
tutto *m / ***tutta** *f* all

U

ubriaco *m / ***ubriaca** *f* drunk
uccello *m* bird
ufficio di cambio *m* currency exchange office
ufficio postale *m* post office
ultimo *m / ***ultima** *f* last
umido *m / ***umida** *f* damp
un sacco *m* a lot
uno one
uomo *m* man
uova strapazzate *f pl* scrambled eggs
uovo *m* egg
usa-e-getta *m / f* disposable
usare to use

uscire to go out
uscire insieme to go out (relationship)
uscita *f* exit, gate (airport)
uva *f* grapes

V

Vaffanculo! @#&! off!
valigia *f* suitcase
valuta *f* currency
Vattene! Go away!
vecchio *m* / **vecchia** *f* old
vedere to see
veloce *m* / *f* fast
velocemente fast
vendere to sell
vendita *f* sale
venire to come
ventilatore *m* fan
vento *m* wind
verde *m* / *f* green

vestiti *m pl* clothes
vetro *m* glass (substance)
viaggiare to travel
viaggio *m* trip; journey
vicino *m* / **vicina** *f* near
vietato *m* / **vietata** *f* forbidden
vigneto *m* vineyard / winery
vincere to win
viola *m* / *f* purple
viso *m* face
vitello *m* veal
vivere to live
voi you (pl.)
volo *m* flight
vongole *f pl* clams
vuoto *m* / **vuota** *f* empty

Z

zaino *m* backpack
zucchero *m* sugar

DICTIONARY
English ▸ Italian

A

to accept accettare
access accesso *m*
accident incidente *m*
account (bank) conto *m*
address (e-mail and postal)
  indirizzo *m*
aerobics aerobica *f*
AIDS AIDS *m*
airmail posta aerea *f*
airport aeroporto *m*
airsickness bag sacchetto per il
  mal d'aria *m*
aisle corsia *f*
amazing incredibile *m / f*
antiseptic antisettico *m*
apartment appartamento *m*
apple mela *f*
to arrest arrestare
arrivals (sign) arrivi *m pl*
to arrive arrivare
artificial sweetener dolcificante *m*
arts (college major) arte *f*
aspirin aspirina *f*
ATM bancomat *m*

B

backpack zaino *m*
bacon pancetta *f*
bad cattivo *m / cattiva f*

bag borsa *f*
baggage bagagli *m pl*
bandage benda *f*
bank banca *f*
bar bar *m*
basketball basket *m*
bass (fish) spigola *f*
bathroom bagno *m*
battery batteria *f*
beach spiaggia *f*
beautiful bello *m / bella f*
bed letto *m*
bedding biancheria da letto *f*
beef manzo *m*
beer birra *f*
beige beige *m / f*
belly button ombelico *m*
bicycle bicicletta *f*
bikini bikini *m*
bill (banknote) banconota *f*
bird uccello *m*
black nero *m / nera f*
blanket coperta *f*
blond biondo *m / bionda f*
blue blu *m / f*
book libro *m*
bookstore libreria *f*
boring noioso *m / noiosa f*
to bother disturbare
bottle bottiglia *f*
boxing boxe *f*
boy ragazzo *m*
boyfriend ragazzo *m*

bra reggiseno *m*

bracelet braccialetto *m*

bread pane *m*

to break down avere un guasto

breakfast colazione *f*

breasts seni *m pl*

briefs un paio di slip *m*

brilliant brillante *m / f*

to bring portare

Britain Gran Bretagna *f*

broken rotto *m / rotta f*

brooch spilla *f*

brother fratello *m*

brown marrone *m / f*

bulimic bulimico *m / bulimica f*

burger hamburger *m*

bus autobus *m*

butter burro *m*

to buy comprare

Bye! Ciao!

C

café caffè *m*

call chiamata *f*

to call chiamare

calorie caloria *f*

camera macchina fotografica *f*

campsite campeggio *m*

Canada Canada *m*

cap (type of hat) berretto *m*

car macchina *f*

car racing gara automobilistica *f*

carafe caraffa *f*

carbonated frizzante *m / f*

card scheda *f*

careful attento *m / attenta f*

carrot carota *f*

cart (luggage) carrello *m*

to cash incassare

casino casinò *m*

castle castello *m*

CD player lettore di CD *m*

cemetery cimitero *m*

chair sedia *f*

change (money) cambio *m*

to change cambiare

charcoal carboncino *m*

chat room chat room *f*

cheap economico *m / economica f*

check (bill) conto *m*

to check in registrarsi

to check out lasciare libera la stanza

checking account conto corrente *m*

cheese formaggio *m*

chicken pollo *m*

chilled freddo *m / fredda f*

chocolate cioccolato *m*

to choke soffocare

cholesterol colesterolo *m*

church chiesa *f*

cigarette sigaretta *f*

class classe *f*

classic rock rock classico *m*

clean pulito *m / pulita f*

to clear (computer, ATM) azzerare

to close chiudere

clothes vestiti *m pl*

clothing store negozio d'abbigliamento *m*

club club, pub *m*

cod merluzzo *m*

coffee caffè *m*

cold freddo *m* / fredda *f*

cold (sickness) raffreddore *m*

color colore *m*

to come venire

commission (fee) commissione *f*

computer computer *m*

concert concerto *m*

conditioner balsamo *m*

condom profilattico *m*

to confirm confermare

confirmation number numero di conferma *m*

consulate consolato *m*

to contact contattare

contraband contrabbando *m*

to cook cucinare

cool (slang) figo *m*

cool (temperature) fresco *m* / fresca *f*

cop poliziotto *m*

corn mais *m*

cosmetics cosmetici *m pl*

to cost costare

cot lettino *m*

cough tosse *f*

cow mucca *f*

cream crema *f*

credit card carta di credito *f*

cucumber cetriolo *m*

cup tazza *f*

currency (foreign) valuta straniera *f*

currency exchange office cambio valuta *m*

cushion cuscino *m*

cycling ciclismo *m*

cyclocross ciclocross *m*

D

to dance ballare

dark scuro *m* / scura *f*

day giorno *m*

decaffeinated coffee caffè decaffeinato *m*

deck chair sedia a sdraio *f*

degree (title) laurea *f*

delayed in ritardo

delicious delizioso *m* / deliziosa *f*

deodorant deodorante *m*

department (in store) reparto *m*

department store grande magazzino *m*

departures partenze *f pl*

deposit deposito *m*

dessert dolce *m*

diabetic diabetico *m* / diabetica *f*

diaphragm diaframma *m*

diarrhea diarrea *f*

diet dieta *f*

digital camera macchina fotografica digitale *f*

dinner cena *f*

dirty sporco *m* / sporca *f*

discount sconto *m*

disease malattia *f*

disgusting schifoso *m* / schifosa *f*

dish piatto *m*

disposable usa-e-getta *m* / *f*

to dive tuffarsi

dive (bar) bettola *f*

doctor dottore *m* / dottoressa *f*

document documento *m*

dollars dollari *m pl*

door porta *f*

download scaricare

downtown area centro città *m*

draft (beer) birra alla spina *f*

to drink bere

drink (alcoholic and non-alcoholic) bevanda *f*

to drip gocciolare

to drive guidare

drugstore farmacia *f*

drunk ubriaco *m* / ubriaca *f*

E

earring orecchino *m*

to eat mangiare

egg uovo *m*

eggplant melanzana *f*

eight otto

e-mail e-mail *f*

emergency emergenza *f*, pronto soccorso *m*

England Inghilterra *f*

English inglese *m* / *f*

to enjoy gustare

enough abbastanza

entrance fee ingresso *m*

equipment equipaggiamento *m*

to exchange cambiare

exchange rate tasso di cambio *m*

excited entusiasta *m* / *f*

to exercise fare ginnastica

to exit uscire

expensive caro *m* / cara *f*

to explain spiegare

exquisite squisito *m* / squisita *f*

extra in più

eyebrow sopracciglio *m*

F

face faccia *f*

facial trattamento del viso *f*

family famiglia *f*

fan (electric) ventilatore *m*

fare tariffa *f*

fast veloce *m* / *f*

fast food fast food *m*

fat grasso *m*

father padre *m*

faucet rubinetto *m*

fever febbre *f*

file (computer) file *m*

to fill riempire

Fire! Al fuoco!

first primo *m* / prima *f*

fish pesce *m*

fitting room camerino *m*

five cinque
flashlight torcia elettrica *f*
flat tire gomma bucata *f*
flea pulce *f*
flight volo *m*
flip-flops ciabatte *f pl*
food cibo *m*
foreign currency valuta straniera *f*
to forget dimenticare
fork forchetta *f*
four quattro
fresh fresco *m* / fresca *f*
fried fritto *m* / fritta *f*
friend amico *m* / amica *f*
fries patatine fritte *f pl*
fruit frutta *f*
furnished apartment
    appartamento ammobiliato *m*

G

gallery galleria *f*
game (sports match) partita *f*
garden giardino *m*
garlic aglio *m*
gas gas *m*
gas station stazione di servizio *f*
gas tank serbatoio *m*
gasoline benzina *f*
gay gay *m* / *f*
to get off scendere
gift shop negozio di regali *m*
girl ragazza *f*
girlfriend ragazza *f*
to give dare

glass (drinking) bicchiere *m*
gluten-free senza glutine
to go andare
to go (food) da asporto
gonorrhea gonorrea *f*
good buono *m* / buona *f*
good morning buon giorno
grapefruit pompelmo *m*
gray grigio *m* / grigia *f*
green verde *m* / *f*
gross disgustoso
guest ospite *m* / *f*
guesthouse pensione *f*
gym palestra *f*

H

hair spray lacca *f*
ham prosciutto *m*
hamburger hamburger *m*
to hang up riattaccare
hang-gliding deltaplano *m*
hangover sbornia *f*
happy felice *m* / *f*
to have avere
hay fever raffreddore da fieno *m*
he lui
headphones cuffie *f pl*
health salute *f*
health food store negozio di
    dietetica *f*
heating system impianto di
    riscaldamento *m*
hello salve
to help aiutare

Help! Aiuto!
here qui
herpes herpes *m*
Hi! Ciao!
hobbies hobby *m*
horrible orribile *m / f*
horse cavallo *m*
hot (temp.) caldo *m /* calda *f,* **(spicy)** piccante *m / f*
hour ora *f*
house casa *f*
How? Come?
to be hungry avere fame

I

ice ghiaccio *m*
ice cream gelato *m*
ice-cream parlor gelateria *f*
included compreso *m /* compresa *f*
information informazione *f*
ingredient ingrediente *m*
insect insetto *m*
insurance assicurazione *f*
interesting interessante *m / f*
International Student Card tessera internazionale per studenti *f*
Internet access accesso a Internet *m*
Internet café Internet café *m*
Ireland Irlanda *f*
itemized bill / check conto dettagliato *m*
IUD spirale *f*

J

jacket giacca *f*
jam marmellata *f*
jet-ski moto acquatica *m*
juice succo *m*
junk food cibo spazzatura *m*

K

key chiave *f*
kiss bacio *m*
to kiss baciare
knife coltello *m*

L

large grande *m / f*
last ultimo *m /* ultima *f*
later più tardi
laundry service servizio lavanderia *f*
least, at almeno
to leave lasciare
lemon limone *m*
lemonade limonata *f*
to lend prestare
lesbian lesbica *f*
lettuce lattuga *f*
life vita *f*
lifeguard bagnino *m*
to lift sollevare
light luce *f*
light beer birra chiara *f*
light (weight) leggero *m /* leggera *f*
link (Web) rimando *m*
lip labbro *m*

liposuction liposuzione f
lipstick rossetto m
liqueur liquore m
liquor store enoteca f
list lista f
to live vivere
lobster aragosta f
local dishes piatti locali m pl
lock serratura f
locker armadietto m
lost perso m / persa f
lost and found oggetti smarriti m pl
loud forte m / f
lover amante m / f
low-calorie ipocalorico m / ipocalorica f
low-cholesterol a basso contenuto di colesterolo
low-fat magro m / magra f
low-sodium a poco contenuto di sodio
luggage bagagli m pl
lunch pranzo m

M

magazine rivista f
mailbox cassetta delle lettere f
make-up trucco m
manager direttore m / direttrice f
map cartina f
market mercato m
marmalade marmellata di agrumi f
mashed potatoes purè di patate m
massage massaggio m

matches fiammiferi m pl
meal pasto m
meat carne f
mechanic meccanico m
memorial monumento m
memory card scheda memoria f
menu menu m
message messaggio m
mileage (per liter) chilometri al litro m pl
milk latte m
milkshake frullato m
mineral water acqua minerale f
mistake errore m
moisturizing cream crema idratante f
money denaro m, soldi m pl
moped motorino m
more ancora, di più
morning mattino m
mother madre f
motion sickness (air) mal d'aria, **(car)** mal d'auto, **(sea)** mal di mare m
motorbike motocicletta f
motorboat barca a motore f
mountain biking ciclismo di montagna m
movie film m
movie theater cinema m
MP3 player lettore di MP3 m
much molto m / molta f
mugging aggressione f

museum museo *m*
mushroom fungo *m*
music musica *f*
mustard senape *f*
my mio *m* / mia *f*, miei *m pl* / mie *f pl*

N

nap (midday) siesta *f*
napkin tovagliolo *m*
nature preserve oasi naturale *f*
near vicino a
nearby vicino *m* / vicina *f*
nearest più vicino
necklace collana *f*
need bisogno *m*
to need avere bisogno
newsstand edicola *f*
next prossimo *m* / prossima *f*
night notte *f*
nightclub locale notturno *m*
nine nove
nipple capezzolo *m*
no no
noisy rumoroso *m* / rumorosa *f*
non-carbonated naturale *m* / *f*
non-smoking area zona non fumatori *f*
nonstop bus autobus senza fermate *m*
nose naso *m*
now adesso
nude beach spiaggia per nudisti *f*
number numero *m*

O

office ufficio *m*
old town città vecchia *f*
on time in orario
one uno
one-way senso unico *m*
onion cipolla *f*
to open aprire
orange (color) arancione *m* / *f*, **(fruit)** arancia *f*
to order ordine *m*
outside fuori

P

package pacco *m*
pain dolore *m*
painkiller analgesico *m*
palace palazzo *m*
panties mutandine *f pl*
paper carta *f*
parents genitori *m pl*
party festa *f*
to party fare festa
passport passaporto *m*
password (online) password *f*
pastry shop pasticceria *f*
to pay pagare
pay phone telefono a scheda *m*
peach pesca *f*
pencil matita *f*
pepper (spice) pepe *m*, **(vegetable)** peperone *m*
per day al giorno

145

per hour all'ora
per night a notte
per week alla settimana
photograph fotografia *f*
pickle sottaceto *m*
pig maiale *m*
pill pillola *f*
pillow cuscino *m*
pineapple ananas *m*
pink rosa *m / f*
plans programmi *m pl*
plastic surgery chirurgia plastica *f*
plate piatto *m*
platform (train station) binario *m*
please per favore
police polizia *f*
pool piscina *f*
pop music musica pop *f*
pork maiale *m*
post office ufficio postale *m*
postage tariffa postale *f*
postcard cartolina *f*
potato patata *f*
pounds (British) sterline *f pl*
prescription ricetta *f*
price prezzo *m*
program of events programma delle manifestazioni *m*
to puke vomitare
purple viola *m / f*
purse borsetta *f*

R

racetrack pista *f*
to raise up alzare
rape stupro *m*
rat ratto *m*
razor blade lametta *f*
receipt ricevuta *f*
to recommend raccomandare
red rosso *m /* rossa *f*
red wine vino rosso *m*
referee arbitro *m*
to rent affittare
to repeat ripetere
to report (to police) denunciare
reservation prenotazione *f*
to reserve prenotare
to restart riaccendere
restaurant ristorante *m*
rice riso *m*
to ride (hitchhiking) passaggio *m*
right of way precedenza *f*
ring anello *m*
rock (music) musica rock *f*
rock climbing scalata *f*
roll (of bread) panino *m*
roll (of toilet paper) rotolo *m* di carta igienica
romantic romantico *m /* romantica *f*
room (hotel) stanza, camera *f*
room service servizio *m* in camera
round trip andata *f* e ritorno *m*

rugby rugby *m*

rum rum *m*

to run into incontrare

S

safe (box) cassaforte *f*

safety sicurezza *f*

salmon salmone *m*

salt sale *m*

sand sabbia *f*

sandal sandalo *m*

sanitary napkin assorbente *m*

satellite TV TV satellitare *f*

savings account conto di risparmio *m*

to say hello/bye salutare

schedule orario *m*

science scienza *f*

Scotland Scozia *f*

scrambled eggs uova strapazzate *f pl*

seat posto *m*

security check controllo di sicurezza *m*

service servizio *m*

set menu menu fisso *m*

seven sette

sex sesso *m*

shampoo sciampo *m*

she lei

shoe scarpa *f*

shop negozio *m*

to go shopping andare a far spese

shopping area zona commerciale *f*

shower doccia *f*

shrimp gambero *m*

sick malato *m* / malata *f*

sickness malattia *f*

side effects effetti collaterali *m pl*

single room stanza singola *f*

sink (bathroom) lavandino *m*

sister sorella *f*

six sei

size (of clothing) taglia *f*

skateboard skateboard *m*

ski sci *m*

skirt gonna *f*

sleeper car cuccetta *f*

sleeping bag sacco a pelo *m*

slippers ciabatte *f pl*

slot machines slot machine *f*

slowly lentamente

small piccolo *m* / piccola *f*

to smoke fumare

smoking area zona fumatori *f*

snack bar bar *m*

sneakers scarpe da ginnastica *f pl*

soap sapone *m*

soccer calcio *m*

sodium sodio *m*

soft drink bibita gassata *f*

sole (fish) sogliola *f*

sore throat mal di gola *m*

sorry spiacente *m* / *f*

so-so così così

sound system sistema acustico *m*

soup zuppa *f*

souvenirs souvenir *m pl*

to speak parlare

speakers altoparlanti *m pl*

special speciale *m / f*

spectacular spettacolare *m / f*

sponge spugna *f*

spoon cucchiaio *m*

sports sport *m pl*

sports fan tifoso *m* / tifosa *f*

sports store negozio di articoli sportivi *m*

sportswear abbigliamento sportivo *m*

squash zucca *f*

stair climber step *m*

stamp (postage) francobollo *m*

station stazione *f*

to stay stare

to steal rubare

steam room bagno turco *m*

to stop fermare

store negozio *m*

strawberry fragola *f*

student studente *m* / studentessa *f*

to study studiare

stunning sensazionale *m / f*

style stile *m*

sublime sublime *m / f*

subway metropolitana *f*

succulent squisito *m* / squisita *f*

sugar zucchero *m*

suitcase valigia *f*

sun sole *m*

sunblock lozione solare *f*

sunburn scottatura *f*

sunstroke insolazione *f*

supermarket supermercato *m*

to surf the Web navigare il Web

surfboard surfboard *m*

to swallow ingoiare

to sweat sudare

sweater maglia *f*

sweet dolce *m / f*

sweetener (artificial) dolcificante *m*

to swim nuotare

swim trunks costume (da bagno) *m*

swimsuit costume (da bagno) *m*

swordfish pesce spada *m*

syphilis sifilide *f*

T

table tavolo *m*

to take prendere

tampon tampone *m*

tank serbatoio *m*

tattoo tatuaggio *m*

taxi taxi *m*

tea tè *m*

telephone telefono *m*

television televisione *f*

ten dieci

tent tenda *f*

terrible terribile *m / f*

thanks grazie

theater teatro *m*

theft furto *m*

there là

they loro
thief ladro m / ladra f
thing cosa f
to be thirsty avere sete
thong tanga m
three tre
throat gola f
ticket biglietto m
tip (for service) mancia f
tire gomma f
tired stanco m / stanca f
toast pane tostato m
today oggi
toilet gabinetto m
tomorrow domani
tonic water acqua tonica f
tonight (evening) stasera,
  (night) stanotte
tooth dente m
toothpaste dentifricio m
tourist turista m
tow truck carro attrezzi m
towel asciugamano m
town città f
track and field atletica f
train treno m
to translate tradurre
translator traduttore m /
  traduttrice f
trash can bidone (della
  spazzatura) m
travelers check travel check m
treadmill tapis roulant m
trip (travel) viaggio m

trout trota f
T-shirt maglietta f
tuna tonno m
turkey tacchino m
to turn off (machine) spegnere
to turn on (machine) accendere
two due

U

ugly brutto m / brutta f
umbrella ombrello m
underdone (food) poco cotto m /
  cotta f
to understand capire
unfurnished apartment
  appartamento vuoto m
United States Stati Uniti m pl

V

vanilla vaniglia f
veal vitello m
vegan vegano m / vegana f
vegetable soup zuppa di verdure f
vegetarian vegetariano m /
  vegetariana f
venereal disease malattia
  venerea f
vinaigrette condimento olio e
  aceto m
vineyard vigneto m
vitamin vitamina f
vodka vodka f
volleyball pallavolo f
to vomit vomitare

W

to wait aspettare
waiter / waitress cameriere *m* / cameriera *f*
waiting room sala d'attesa *f*
to wake up svegliarsi
Wales Galles *m*
wallet portafogli *m*
water acqua *f*
to wax (hair) depilare
we noi
web page pagina web *f*
web site sito web *m*
week settimana *f*
weekend fine settimana *m*
weightlifting sollevamento pesi *m*
What? Cosa?
When? Quando?
Where? Dove?
white bianco *m* / bianca *f*
Who? Chi?
Why? Perché?

Wi-Fi® wi-fi® *m*
to win vincere
window finestra *f*
wine vino *m*
winery cantina *f*
with con
to withdraw ritirare
withdrawal (of money) prelievo *m*
without senza
to work (machine) funzionare
to work (occupation) lavorare
worm verme *m*
wrestling (free style) lotta libera *f*
wristwatch orologio da polso *m*
to write scrivere

Y

yellow giallo *m* / gialla *f*
yes sì
youth hostel ostello della gioventù *m*